THE SAGA OF TEXAS COOKERY

THE SAGA OF TEXAS COOKERY

AN HISTORICAL GUIDE OF MORE THAN ONE HUNDRED TWENTY RECIPES ILLUSTRATING THE FRENCH INFLUENCE ON TEXAS CUISINE, THE SPANISH INFLUENCE, & THE MEXICAN, INCLUDING ALSO CONTRIBUTIONS FROM THE EUROPEAN SETTLERS IN THE REPUBLIC OF TEXAS & FROM THE RESOURCEFUL SOUTHERNERS DURING THE CONFEDERACY, AS WELL AS FROM TEXANS OF EVERY SORT RIGHT DOWN TO THE PRESENT. BY SARAH MORGAN

1981 : TEXIAN PRESS : WACO

First Printing, 1973
Second Printing, 1981

ISBN 0-88426-032-1

Published
by

Waco, Texas

FOREWORD

THE SIX FLAGS which have waved proudly over Texas have left their marks, not only on the social, economic, and political character of the state, but on its food and eating habits as well. Texas has one of the most interesting and most varied cuisines in the world. It is the only state in the Union that can boast of a cuisine that is a delightful mixture of French, Spanish, Mexican, and Deep Southern, seasoned with the finesse which was the contribution made by the European immigrants to the New Republic.

To really understand Texas food, one must know something of the land and the people. It is often as simple and as forceful as the staunch old cowboy; as full of variety as the landscape; as generous as the vast expanse of the ranch country; as delectable as the citrus valley; and more often good than otherwise.

The differences of climate, culture, topography, art, dress, language, foods, and means of livelihood would appear to make the state a divisive place in which to live. However, with all of these apparent extremes the population has managed to blend itself into a workable and cohesive society, and one of the most powerful of the amalgamating forces of this blend is the *food*.

Unfortunately, the average tourist seldom reaps the benefits of this heritage and he may not even be aware of it, as he travels over the vast stretch of our highways. People often identify barbecue, hamburgers, chicken-fried steak, pinto beans, fried chicken, and enchiladas as typical Texas foods. Although all of these can be found throughout the state, they are only typical of the highway foods.

The best and most exciting Texas foods are found in the homes, or in obscure and little-publicized restaurants and in the more elegant and more expensive restaurants of our larger cities, such as Houston, San Antonio, Dallas, Fort Worth, and many others.

This book is not a travel guide to the eating places of Texas. It is rather an attempt to make available to the readers some of the exciting food history and recipes which came about directly or indirectly through the influence of the potpourri beginning of this giant state.

Sarah Morgan
Fort Worth, Texas

ACKNOWLEDGEMENT

MY SINCERE THANKS to Dr. W. C. Nunn, Professor of History at Texas Christian University, Fort Worth, Texas, for his excellent help in reading, advising and guiding in the preparation of the history comments in this manuscript.

CONTENTS

TEXAS UNDER THE CONFEDERACY : 41

THE UNION FOREVER : 53

THE SAGA OF TEXAS COOKERY

ABOUT THE RECIPES

IN KEEPING with the flavor and romance of Texas history, this book includes several recipes, or "receipts" as they were called for many years, just as they were published some hundred years or more ago, using the unique language, quaint measurements, and regional expressions. Also included are my own collection, gathered from friends whose forefathers were among the early settlers; others I have acquired by living in immigrant settlements, and many of the *here-and-now* type will bring Texas cookery up to date.

Some of the recipes handed down by our forefathers or foremothers were masterpieces of creative ingenuity. Early-day Texas cooks made great contributions to present-day cookery and eating habits by their miraculous imagination and thrift in making use of new or limited supplies of food. The reader may discover some overlapping or at least similarities in the recipes; although Texas was settled by people from many different countries and the state's history covers hundreds of years, the basic and available foods remain the same.

You will find the recipes arranged under the historical flag which most nearly identifies them as to their origin or which influenced their beginning.

THE FRENCH IN TEXAS

THE FIRST FLAG to fly over Texas, or the territory which the Indians called Tejas, was the *French*. Although France's official reign was short, her colonists were in the state many years before and many years afterward. LaSalle established a colony in southeastern Texas as early as 1685. Then many years later, about 1817, a colony made up of exiles from the army of the great Napoleon settled at the mouth of the Trinity River.

The early French settlers—as did most other early immigrants—brought with them from Europe traditional ideas of their cooking and applied them to the native foodstuffs. This made an unusual and fascinating combination and created one of the most distinct cuisines to be found anywhere. The swampy Gulf coast was ideally suited to raise rice, which soon became one of the staple starches of their diet, along with the corn obtained from the Indians.

The abundance of shellfish found in the Gulf made an excellent beginning for the oyster stews and shrimp gumbos and rice dishes combined with fish. Then later, the many creole dishes which are still in great evidence in this area came into existence through a combination of the French and Spanish cookery.

Louisiana is often given credit for being the center of exquisite creole dishes. This is only partially true. The authentic creole cuisine, which is a magic blend of French and Spanish, is certainly an end-product of original affection and imagination no matter where it is found.

5

THE FRENCH & THEIR COFFEE

THE CUSTOM of the French pioneers drinking black and very strong coffee immediately before or just after arising each morning was observed with fervor. If a *slug* of brandy was added it was said to have not only kept chills and fever away but insured longevity as well. To them, coffee was not a luxury but a necessity and it had to be *strong*. One cup of the "ordinary mill" coffee was often used to four cups of boiling water. This was known as *day and night* coffee. The *day* coffee was that which they drank immediately upon arising in the morning and was said to have been strong enough to speak for itself. The *night* coffee, which they drank just before retiring, was made of weaker proportions. During the day they consumed a great deal of whatever happened to be available.

The following is what the French called a *rule* for coffee making and which is still used in many sections of the state today:

FRENCH COFFEE: CAFÉ A LA CREOLE

TO MAKE 4 full-cup servings: Bring 5 cups of water to a boil in a kettle that is to be used for the making. Add 5 tablespoons regular grind coffee and 2 tablespoons chicory. Cover the kettle, set off the flame until it has steeped three or four minutes. Drop in an egg shell, add a sprinkle of salt and 2 tablespoons cold water. Let it rest another two or three minutes. Strain, reheat and drink!!

CREME AU CAFÉ

TO MAKE about 4 servings: Bring to a boil 1/4 cup finely ground coffee in 2 cups sweet milk. Add 1 cup sweet cream, 3 egg yolks beaten with 1/3 cup powdered sugar. Let the mixture simmer until the liquid has reduced about one-fourth. Remove from heat and strain. Serve hot or cold. (Try adding a healthy dash of brandy or bourbon to this recipe. Super!)

CREAM COFFEE JELLY—1836

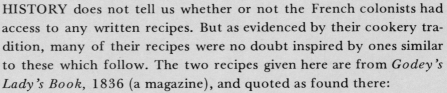

HISTORY does not tell us whether or not the French colonists had access to any written recipes. But as evidenced by their cookery tradition, many of their recipes were no doubt inspired by ones similar to these which follow. The two recipes given here are from *Godey's Lady's Book*, 1836 (a magazine), and quoted as found there:

Boil an ounce of coffee berries, 25 coriander seeds, 1/2 stick cinnamon, a bit of orange peel, and a little loaf sugar in a pint of good cream for nearly one-fourth hour. In the meantime having beat up the whites of 4 eggs, strain to them the warm liquid, put all over the fire, keep whisking it 'till it thickens and then pour it into a dish or separate cups or glasses and serve it up cold with any favorite biscuits. Some prepare an agreeable coffee cream by making a gill of very strong and clear coffee and a pint of rich calf's foot jelly which they mix together while both are hot, adding a pint of good cream with loaf or Lisbon sugar to suit the palate. As this will jelly, though it should not be stiff, it is as much entitled to be called coffee jelly as the coffee cream.

(Try it! You won't like it!)

BOIL an ounce of the best scraped chocolate in a pint of rich cream and a pint of good milk with a quarter of a pound of loaf sugar. When milled quite smooth, take it off the fire; and while it cools whisk up the whites of 6 or 8 eggs; put it into glasses, take the froth of the eggs with a spoon, lay it on sieves, then put it into the glasses so as for some of it to rise above the cream and thus serve it up.

CHOCOLATE CREAM—1836

CUSTARDS, which have always been an important part of the French cuisine, took many forms in the early days of our history. The following recipe found in an early edition of *The White House Cookbook* (first published in 1887), is a good example of how simple ingredients were turned into an elegant dessert.

A quote from a 1915 edition of *The White House Cookbook:*

Boil a quart of milk; when boiling stir into it the well beaten yolks of six eggs; add six tablespoons sugar and one tablespoonful of sifted flour, which has been well beaten together; when boiled turn it into a dish and pour over it the whites beaten to a stiff froth, mixing with them six tablespoonsful of powdered sugar. Set all in the oven and brown slightly. Flavor the top with vanilla and the bottom with lemon. Serve cold.

GOLDEN CREAM— 1887 STYLE

THE FAMOUS POT of Jambalaya is an excellent example of the French influence in making use of several available foods in one marvelous dish. It may be served under different names, but the delicate seasonings of aromatic herbs will be in any and all of them. Shrimp and oysters may be used as a base or perhaps chicken and oysters, with bacon or ham, or a combination of all. And the cook may have his own opinion on which combination is best; he may

THE FRENCH JAMBALAYA

r

modify the ingredients and the seasonings according to his temper, the weather, or his state of health on that particular day. The following recipe I consider not only basic but very excellent:

JAMBALAYA: HAM & SHRIMP

TO MAKE 4 to 6 servings: Melt 3 tablespoons shortening over low heat. Stir in 1 tablespoon flour and cook until the flour is slightly brown. Add 1/4 pound baked and cubed ham, 1/2 cup minced green peppers, 1 bay leaf, 1/2 teaspoon thyme, 1 tablespoon minced fresh parsley, 1/2 cup finely chopped onion, and 1 minced garlic clove. Cook the mixture slowly until the onion and peppers are tender. Salt and pepper to taste. Next pour into the mixture 2 cups of canned tomatoes and 1 cup of the tomato juice. Allow the mixture to simmer for about ten minutes. Stir occasionally. Just a few minutes before time to serve add one pound of shrimp, which has been cleaned and deveined; cook over low heat just until the shrimp are pink. Have 1 cup of rice cooked, according to directions, and while it is still very hot, serve this delectable mixture over it.

GUMBO FILÉ

MANY of the old-timers in the French-influenced section of Texas still abide by the rule of adding sassafras powder to their gumbo recipes. It is added just after the gumbo has cooked and just before it is served. It thickens the gumbo. The Choctaw Indians prepared the herb by drying the leaves, then pounding them into a powder on a stone mortar. The powder is called gumbo filé and can be purchased in most supermarkets today. The gumbo may be thickened by using okra instead of the filé, or the okra may be an addition.

CREOLE GUMBO: CHICKEN & OYSTER

THE CHICKEN used in the following recipe may be boned after it is cooked; however, the early settlers served it in this manner to save time and energy in its preparation:

To make 8 to 10 servings: Cut one 2-pound chicken into serving pieces. Sprinkle with salt and pepper to taste, then dredge in flour. In a large heavy kettle or skillet, with fitting lid, melt 4 tablespoons butter, add 1/4 pound sliced and diced salt pork and bring to the frying point. Drop in the chicken pieces and fry for about 20 minutes, turning to brown on all sides. Next add 1/2 cup chopped onion, 1 bay leaf, 1/2 teaspoon thyme, and 1/4 teaspoon cayenne pepper. Shake the kettle to distribute the seasonings. Add one quart of oyster stock and 2 cups of boiling water. Cover and cook slowly for about one hour or until the chicken is very tender. When almost ready to serve add two dozen oysters, fresh or canned, and simmer three or four minutes. Just before serving remove the gumbo from the heat and stir in 2 tablespoons gumbo filé. Do not allow the gumbo to boil after the filé has been added. It may be served over hot rice or in a bowl with some rice added to the soup-like mixture.

CRAB ÉTOUFFÉE

ÉTOUFFÉE literally means "smothered" and in this instance be sure to make a generous amount of this thick rich sauce and "étouffée" the crab.

To make 4 to 6 servings: In a large saucepan blend 4 tablespoons melted butter with 4 tablespoons flour and cook over low heat until slightly brown. Add 1 cup finely chopped onions, 1/2 cup finely chopped celery, and 1 teaspoon finely chopped garlic clove. Cook slowly until all ingredients are tender. Add 2 cups canned tomatoes— the peeled variety—drained and chopped, 1 tablespoon Worcestershire sauce, and 1/4 teaspoon cayenne pepper. Salt to taste. Cook for about five minutes over low heat, then pour in 2 cups freshly made fish stock, or if fish stock is not available, substitute chicken stock. Simmer this mixture for about 20 minutes. Just before time to serve, add 2 cups fresh—or frozen—crab meat and simmer until the crab is thoroughly hot. Taste for seasoning and serve on a mound of rice which has been freshly cooked and is steaming hot.

or if

DIRTY RICE

ONE of the *most* regional of the recipes: (And don't let the name mislead you; it isn't dirty at all. In fact, this recipe makes a wonderful dish to be used either as a stuffing for fowl or served just as an entrée.)

To make 6 to 8 servings: Cook 2 cups rice according to package directions and set aside. Boil one pound of chicken giblets, or giblets from any fowl, in water to cover. To this add 1/2 cup chopped onions, 1 chopped garlic clove, and salt to taste. When the giblets are tender, drain them and grind through a food chopper. Save the broth in which the giblets were cooked to use later. In 2 tablespoons butter sauté 1/2 cup chopped green pepper, 1/2 cup chopped celery, 1/2 cup chopped onion, and 1/2 teaspoon thyme until all ingredients are tender. Combine the mixtures with the rice and add sufficient broth to moisten well. Pour the mixture into a buttered baking pan and bake at 350° until slightly brown, about 30 minutes.

RICE CREOLE

THERE are as many rice creole recipes as there are cooks to make them. However, I believe that no book of this nature would be complete without including at least one of this type.

To make 4 to 6 servings: Cook 1 cup of rice according to package directions and set aside. Sauté 1/4 cup minced onion and 1/2 cup diced celery in 2 tablespoons butter until tender. Season with 1/2 teaspoon thyme, 1 bay leaf, salt and pepper to taste, and a sprinkle of ground cloves. Next stir in 2 cups canned tomatoes and 1 cup meat stock. Simmer over low heat until mixture is well blended and slightly reduced in amount, about 15 minutes. Combine the sauce with the rice and simmer for another 10 minutes. Serve at once.

OYSTER SAUSAGE

THIS SAUSAGE RECIPE is a "hear-say," and I have never tried to make it, but I "hear-say" it is excellent. Why don't you try it?

To make 4 to 6 servings: Chop 6 or 8 slightly cooked oysters into rather small pieces. Add 1 pound of ground veal and mix with 1 egg, salt and pepper to taste, and just enough bread crumbs to hold the mixture together. Form into oblong sausage-like cakes, dip them in bread crumbs, and fry in hot bacon fat.

CABBAGE GUMBO

TO MAKE 6 to 8 servings: In a large saucepan, heat 2 tablespoons bacon fat, add 1/2 cup chopped onion, and sauté until tender. Add 1/2 pound lean, tender steak, cut into cubes, 1/2 pound baked ham, cut into small pieces, and 1/2 pound highly seasoned sausage. Cook the meats over medium heat until the steak is tender and slightly brown. Stir and shake the saucepan while the meats are cooking to prevent sticking. Shred one large head of fresh, crisp cabbage, using some of the green leaves with the white ones, then add to the meat mixture. Cover and cook over low heat, adding a little water as needed to keep the mixture moist, stirring occasionally, until all ingredients are tender. Do not overcook! Just before serving, add 1 pimiento, cut into narrow strips, a sprinkle of cayenne pepper, and serve very hot. The gumbo may not need salt, since the sausage will add this seasoning; however, one should taste for seasonings and add whatever is desired.

THESE GRIDDLE CAKES are still found at times in parts of Southeast Texas, and are often served with a generous helping of what the natives call "home-made sorghum":

To make 4 to 6 servings: Mash 1 cup of canned hominy through a sieve and stir in 1 1/2 cups buttermilk. Beat 3 eggs until light and add to the mixture. Melt 1/4 cup butter, stir in 2 tablespoons sugar, and 1/2 teaspoon salt. Combine the mixtures and stir until smooth. Sift 3/4 cup flour with 1/2 teaspoon soda and 2 teaspoons baking powder and combine all the mixtures. Blend well by beating by hand. The batter should be thick enough to hold its shape when dropped by spoonsful onto a hot griddle. Bake on a hot griddle and serve with home-made sorghum.

ONCE I read in an old cookbook some directions which went something like this: "Very early in the morning make a batter of flour, warm milk, and yeast, and let rise 'til time to make the *flannel* breakfast cakes. . . ." Obviously these directions were not given for the cooks of our present-day society. The name *flannel* cakes was used for breakfast cakes made with yeast for the rising quality instead of soda or baking powder.

Now for a modern version of these unusual cakes and to make 6 to 8 servings: Scald 2 cups sweet milk, add 1 teaspoon salt, 6 tablespoons butter, 2 tablespoons sugar. Set aside to cool. When the mixture cools to room temperature, stir in one package of yeast. Add 1 1/2 cups flour and stir until smooth. Cover with a cloth and set aside in a warm place for about 20 minutes. Beat 3 egg yolks until light and add to the yeast mixture. Next, beat the 3 egg whites until stiff and fold into the batter. Drop by spoonsful onto a hot buttered griddle and bake as you would any batter cakes. If time permits, you may let the batter rise for one hour or longer. These are wonderfully light cakes and can be served with bacon, ham, syrup, or as you would any pancake.

TO MAKE 6 servings: Take 6 slices of dry or stale *French* bread, (other bread may be used but it will not be as good). Scald 2 cups sweet milk with 1/3 cup sugar, then cool slightly. Add 2 tablespoons brandy and lay the bread in it to soak for about 10 minutes. A shallow baking pan is best for this procedure. Drain the bread well and

11 : THE FRENCH IN TEXAS

set aside. Beat the yolks of 4 eggs and whites separately. Combine the two mixtures with 2 tablespoons sugar and the grated rind of one lemon. Soak the bread in this mixture for about another 10 minutes. Remove to a well buttered cookie sheet and bake in a hot oven, 450° until brown, about 15 minutes. Delicious!

BEIGNETS: FRENCH DOUGHNUTS

THESE DOUGHNUTS are sometimes called "dunkin' doughnuts" because they are made in squares and therefore are easily dunked into the hot cup of coffee. "Dunkin' " hasn't always been considered the most admirable of eating habits, but it is really fun with these doughnuts. Try it!

To make about 2 dozen doughnuts: Pour 1/2 cup boiling water over 2 tablespoons shortening, 1/4 cup sugar, 1/2 teaspoon salt, and set aside. Soften 1/2 package yeast in 1/4 cup warm water with 1 teaspoon sugar and set aside. In a large mixing bowl beat 1 egg until light, add 1/2 cup undiluted evaporated milk. Stir well, then combine all mixtures. Beat by hand and little by little add about 3 1/4 cups flour. The batter should be very thick, but not too thick to stir. Cover and set in the refrigerator to chill for at least 30 minutes. On a lightly floured board roll the dough out to about 1/2 inch thickness, and cut into squares. Use a small amount of the dough at a time to make handling easier. Fry a few at a time in deep hot fat, turning to brown on all sides. Drain on absorbent paper and sprinkle generously with confectioners sugar. *Happy dunkin'.*

FRENCH BREAD

THIS FRENCH BREAD recipe is a very simple one to make and although it may not rival the *poor boy* version found in New Orleans, it is a most satisfying one.

To make 2 medium-size loaves: Dissolve 1 package yeast in 1 1/4 cups warm water with 1 teaspoon sugar. Stir into this mixture 2 teaspoons salt, 1 tablespoon sugar, 1 tablespoon shortening, and approximately 3 1/4 cups flour. The dough should be thick enough to knead but not heavy. Knead on a lightly floured board until light and elastic. Place in a greased bowl, brush with melted butter over top, cover, and let rise until double in bulk. When the dough has doubled punch it down and divide into two parts. Roll out, or in some manner form a long thin roll with tapered ends. Place the loaves, fold side down, on a greased baking sheet. Sprinkle each with cornmeal and brush with a cornstarch glaze. The glaze is made with 1 teaspoon corn-starch, 1 tablespoon cold water, blended until smooth, and then poured into 1/2 cup boiling water. Cook this mixture over low heat until smooth and blended, about 3 or 4 minutes. Cool the glaze slightly before brushing the loaves. Let the loaves rise, covered or un-covered, until almost doubled in bulk, about one hour or a little longer. Brush again with the glaze, and make 1/4 inch slashes—on an angle—on each loaf at 2 to 3 inch intervals. A pan of boiling water should be placed in the oven immediately under the bread. Place the loaves in a preheated oven, 400°, and bake for 10 minutes. Remove and brush again with the glaze, return to the oven and continue to bake at 400° for about 30 minutes, or until the loaves are brown. Remove from oven and pan, brush with butter—and *eat!*

THE SPANIARDS IN TEXAS

AFTER the French rule came the Spanish. From 1528 when Cabeza de Vaca was shipwrecked on the shores of Texas, the Spanish were some part, often a very small part, of Texas until 1821. In 1690 when the first Spanish missionaries came into East Texas, they found several different tribes of Indians. They were raising corn, beans, and melons. It is recorded that Indians entertained the priests with their dances and fed them well on *tamales* and *mush*. People often think of the tamale as having been introduced by Mexico, but Texas history mentions many times the Indians feeding the colonists these foods along with corn, peppers, and wild game. It is possible that the tamales which the Indians in Texas taught the Spaniards to make were made with different seasonings from those made in Mexico.

It seems that corn was the most important and the most plentiful food in this period of history. However, later in the life of the Spanish pioneers they began to use more rice and less corn in their cookery. And although these pioneers were most grateful for the corn and its many uses, not everyone liked it or any part of it. One visiting diplomat from England is said to have written home that eating cornbread was like eating cooked sawdust.

During this period in Texas history there was an abundance of game: wild horses (which the settlers were often forced to eat), cattle, turkeys, buffalo, deer, and antelope by the herds. The woods were full of wild grapes, plums, persimmons and berries. Various nuts were to be found in large quantities along the streams, such as hickory nuts and pecans.

15

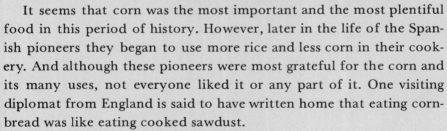

Spanish and Mexican foods have often been thought of as being one and the same. There are a number of overlapping spots in the two cuisines. It could be said also that the French, Spanish, and Mexican foods overlapped in many instances. In fact, there are times when you might think that the Spaniards were squeezed out of the food picture and only the Mexican and the French got the credits.

It is true, however, that after a time the Spanish foods became basically fish, rice, wild game and were seasoned with very subtle touches of various herbs, a great deal like the French seasonings. The Mexicans emphasized the corn and meat combinations, with the eternal chilis and other bold and exciting herbs such as the comino seeds, coriander, and garlic.

The Spanish colonists may have based their cookery on just such fascinating directions and ingredients as the two recipes which follow. These are actual recipes—given in free translation—from an old sixteenth century Spanish cookbook, *Libra de Guisado*, first published in Madrid, 1529:

PASTEL DE CABRITO: PIE MADE OF KID—1529

IF THE KID is too fat to roast, cut it into pieces and make pies. Make a sauce of cut up perejil (parsley) and put in the pies with a little sweet oil and place it in the oven. A little before you take it out of the oven beat some eggs with vinegar or orange juice and put into the pie through the holes made in the crust for the steam to escape. Then return pies to oven for enough time to repeat *The Lord's Prayer three times*, then take the pies out and put them before the master of the house, cut it and give it to him.

SALSA BLANCA: WHITE SAUCE—1529

TAKE raw ginger and peel off the skin so that it is white; chop into little pieces. Put it to soak for part of the night in fine rose water. In the morning you will take well blanched and white almonds and mash them well in a mortar. Make a paste of the almonds with egg yolks and mix it with chicken broth which has been well salted, and put it through a strainer. Then put this milk into the pot in which it is to be cooked. Take whole canela (cinnamon) and tie it with a string and put it in boiling chicken broth with some cloves, which are scalded in the same way. After the sauce is about half cooked put the canela and the cloves in the pot with the ginger soaked in the rose water. If there does not seem to be enough ginger put in a little ground ginger, because this sauce *wants to know the ginger a little and rose water more.* Moreover, the rose water ought not to be added until all is boiling, and afterwards the sauce is to be poured into plate cups and then sprinkled with fine sugar.

THE PIONEER COOKS made many corn recipes to be used either as a custard or as a bread. The following recipe is an example of this combination. The spider was a special shape skillet or baking pan. The recipe given here is one taken from a 1915 edition of the old 1887 *White House Cookbook:*

Beat two eggs and one-fourth cup sugar together. Then add one cup sweet milk and one cup of sour milk in which you have dissolved one teaspoonful soda. Add a teaspoonful of salt. Then mix one and two-thirds cups of granulated corn meal and one-third cup flour with this. Put a spider skillet on the range and when it is hot melt in two tablespoonsful of butter. Turn the spider so that the butter can run up on the sides of the pan. Pour in the corn cake mixture and add one more cup of sweet milk, but do not stir afterwards. Put this in the oven and bake from twenty to thirty-five minutes. When done there should be a streak of custard through it.

This unusual corn cake can be served with molasses or a sprinkle of brown sugar, or both.

JAMBALAYA, which is both a Spanish and a French creation, or more often a combination of both, deserves special attention no matter where it is found in our food history. This is why you find it here and in the French section.

To make 4 to 6 servings: Cut 1 pound of fresh pork into small pieces, salt and pepper them, and set aside. In 2 tablespoons melted butter sauté 1/2 cup minced onion, 1 minced garlic clove, and 4 tablespoons chopped parsley over low heat until the onions are tender. Add 1/2 teaspoon thyme, 1 bay leaf, 1/4 teaspoon cayenne pepper, and 1/2 teaspoon ground cloves. Stir until the mixture is well blended. Add to this mixture 2 cups of beef broth, combine with the diced pork and simmer for about 30 minutes or until the meat is very tender. Serve over a mound of freshly cooked hot rice. One cup of uncooked rice, cooked according to package directions, should be sufficient to serve 4 to 6 persons.

17 : THE SPANIARDS IN TEXAS

HAM CREOLE

TO MAKE about 4 servings: Cut 1/2 pound of baked or boiled ham into thin strips and set aside. In 2 tablespoons of melted butter stir in 2 tablespoons flour and cook slowly until the mixture is smooth and slightly brown. Add 1 bay leaf, 1/4 teaspoon cayenne pepper, 1/2 teaspoon thyme, 1/2 cup minced onion, 1/2 cup thin strips of green pepper, and 1/4 cup minced pimiento. Cook the mixture over low heat until all ingredients are tender. Add 2 cups of chicken stock and the ham and simmer for about 20 minutes. Salt the mixture with caution since the ham will be salty already. Have 1 cup of rice cooked and hot. Serve the creole over the rice, or combine them and serve in a bowl as you would a thick soup.

SPANISH OMELET: TOMATO & ONION

TO MAKE 4 servings: In 2 tablespoons of hot butter sauté 1/4 cup minced onion and 1 large fresh tomato, peeled and chopped, until the onion is tender. Season with salt and cayenne pepper to taste. Set aside in a pan of hot water while the eggs are being prepared. Beat 4 egg yolks until light, fold in 2 tablespoons of flour, sprinkle with salt and blend well. Beat the whites of 4 eggs until stiff and fold them into the yolk mixture. Have a large skillet ready with 2 tablespoons of butter hot enough to bubble but not to brown. Pour the eggs into this, tilt and turn the skillet to distribute the eggs evenly while they are cooking—two or three minutes. When they are almost done, spread the onion and tomato mixture over them, then fold the omelet in the center. Cook just long enough to absorb the remaining liquid, but do not allow the omelet to become dry. Serve immediately on hot plates or a hot platter. Thin strips of green peppers make a nice garnish for this delicious dish.

ROAST WILD GOOSE: HUNTER'S STYLE

TO SERVE 10 to 12 persons: The goose should weigh from 12 to 14 pounds after it is dressed. When you are ready to cook the goose, place it in a large kettle with 1 onion, chopped, 1 cup vinegar, 2 tablespoons salt and water to cover. Boil slowly for about 20 minutes. Remove it from the water and rinse well. Next place it in a large roaster with 6 or 8 cups of water, sprinkle generously with salt and black pepper. Lay thin slices of onion and apples over the breast of the goose. Roast, covered, at 375° for three or four hours, depending on the tenderness of the bird. About 30 minutes before the goose has finished roasting, baste it with a mixture of 1/2 cup port wine and 1/2 cup broth from the bird. A stuffing may be made of cornbread, chopped celery, apples, onions, black walnuts, and seasonings.

FRIED BEAN ROLL

PREPARE a day or so ahead of serving time a generous amount of dry beans, either the pinto or the red bean. They should be well seasoned while being cooked with grated onion and bacon fat and cooked until almost dry. After they are done drain them well, season with mashed chilis. Pour them into a skillet which has sufficient bacon fat to prevent sticking; mash and cook until the beans are a smooth, dry blend. Remove from fire and when cool enough to handle, form into a roll about three inches in diameter. Chill for several hours. When ready to use, cut the roll into rounds about one inch thick and drop into hot bacon fat. Turn once or twice while frying. They should be slightly brown and served very hot. These can be flattened slightly and used in sandwiches. Excellent!!!

SPANISH RICE: OLD STYLE

TO MAKE 4 to 6 servings: Cook 1 1/2 cups rice according to package directions. It should be very light and very fluffy when cooked. In a saucepan melt 2 tablespoons butter and add 1/2 cup minced onion, 1/2 cup minced green peppers, 1/3 cup minced pimiento, and 1/2 cup finely chopped celery. Sauté until all ingredients are tender. Season with 1/4 teaspoon cayenne pepper, salt to taste, and add 1 cup chicken or beef broth. Combine the mixtures and pour into a well-buttered casserole. Sprinkle the top with bacon fat and bake at 350° for about 30 minutes or until slightly brown. Serve very hot.

INDIAN MEAL PUDDING

TO MAKE 6 to 8 servings: Scald 3 cups sweet milk and set aside. Blend together 6 tablespoons cornmeal, 1 teaspoon cinnamon, 1/4 teaspoon nutmeg, 1/2 teaspoon ginger, and 2 tablespoons sugar. Pour the dry mixture slowly into the warm milk and stir until blended. Add 3 tablespoons molasses, 1 beaten egg, 2 tablespoons melted butter, and blend well. Pour the batter into a well-greased baking dish, set it in a pan of hot water, and bake in a slow oven, 325°, for about 2 hours. During the first half hour of baking stir the batter two or three times. After the mixture has baked about 1 hour, pour in 1/2 cup sweet milk and continue baking but do not stir. The pudding should be dark, rich and of a coarse texture. Serve hot or cold with either whipped cream or a dollop of sour cream.

19 : THE SPANIARDS IN TEXAS

RICE BREAKFAST CAKES

THIS UNUSUAL MIXTURE of yeast and rice is seldom found anymore except in homes where the influence of the forefathers is still felt and cherished. In the early days of our history the maids in the homes would make these, deep-fry them, and then take them out on the street, while they were still very hot, and sell them!

To make 6 to 8 servings: The night before these cakes are to be served, dissolve 1 package yeast in 1/2 cup warm water. Mash well 3 cups of cooked, moist rice, add the yeast and 1 tablespoon sugar. Cover this mixture and let rise over-night. In the morning beat 3 eggs until light, add 1/2 cup sugar, 3 tablespoons flour, or a little more, 1/4 teaspoon nutmeg, and mix well. Set aside again to rise for about 20 minutes. Butter a hot griddle and drop by tablespoons, cooking as you would any griddle cake. Drain on paper towels and serve with bacon, ham or syrup.

PERSIMMON PUDDING

TEXAS HISTORY tells us that the Spanish pioneers were making a persimmon pudding and much to the delight of the hearty male population they made a powerful persimmon beer. I couldn't find a beer recipe but here's the persimmon pudding:

Run sufficient ripe—very ripe—persimmons through a sieve to make 2 cups purée. Cream 1/2 cup butter and 2 cups sugar. Add 3 well-beaten eggs and blend well. Sift 2 cups flour with 1 teaspoon soda, 1 teaspoon baking powder, 1/2 teaspoon allspice, and 1/2 teaspoon cloves. Add the dry ingredients alternately with 2 cups sweet milk to the egg mixture and persimmons. Mix well but do not beat. Pour into a greased pan and bake at 350° for about 35 minutes or until the pudding tests done. A shallow pan of water may be put in the oven with the pudding as it bakes to keep it moist. Cool slightly before removing from the pan. Serve sprinkled with powdered sugar.

MOLASSES PIE

THE SPANISH SETTLERS learned to make a sweet syrup from a certain species of corn by pressing the stalks. Perhaps this sweet syrup was a forerunner of our country molasses. This pie recipe using country molasses has been around for a long time.

For one 9-inch pie prepare the unbaked pie crust and set aside. Blend 1 tablespoon flour, 1/2 cup sugar, 3 eggs and 2 tablespoons vinegar together. Stir until smooth, then add 1 cup country molasses, or sorghum, and 1 cup chopped pecan meats. Pour into the unbaked crust and bake at 400º for 15 minutes; then reduce the heat to 325º and bake for about 45 minutes or until the pie is slightly brown and well set.

THE NUMBER of cookies this recipe will make depends upon the size you choose to make them.

SWEET POTATO COOKIES

Beat 3/4 cup shortening with 1 cup sugar and 2 eggs until the mixture is smooth and light. Stir in 2 cups mashed cooked sweet potatoes, 1 teaspoon vanilla, 1/2 teaspoon salt, 1 teaspoon cinnamon, 1/2 teaspoon nutmeg, and 1/2 cup chopped pecan meats. Mix until well blended. Sift 2 cups flour with 2 teaspoons baking powder and 1/4 teaspoon soda. Add gradually to the sweet potato mixture. The mixture should be a thick batter but thin enough to drop from a spoon. Use more or less flour to get the desired thickness. On a well-greased cookie sheet drop the batter from a teaspoon about 2 inches apart. Bake in a hot oven, 375º, for about 20 minutes or until done.

TO MAKE approximately 18 punch-cup servings: Dissolve 1 cup sugar in 1 cup water and stir in 3 tablespoons lemon or lime juice, 2 cups orange juice, and 4 cups dry red wine. Chill and serve with ice chunks added. For an added "zip" include 1/2 cup good brandy.

SANGRÍA: WINE PUNCH

THE MEXICANS IN TEXAS

THE NEXT FLAG to be unfurled over Texas was the Mexican. Mexico gained her independence from Spain in 1821 and immediately rushed up to take Texas away from the Spanish. Her reign lasted until 1836, and although her political control ended then, her culture, food, eating habits, and her art are still very much a part of the social and cultural life of the Lone Star State.

Mexico contributed many wonderful and lasting food ideas to our heritage of cookery, among them the bold and exciting seasonings of chilis, comino seeds, garlic, coriander, oregano, and many others. Corn, chilis, and beans were among the most basic of the Mexican foods. Another important food product mentioned during this time as having been introduced to Texas by the Mexicans was cocoa (chocolate) from the cacao tree which is native to Mexico.

Many of the old and excellent Mexican cooks still insist that the full flavor of good Mexican cookery depends on doing everything as in the old days—when the women worked slowly with their hands and with very little or very simple equipment. Corn, they will say, is never just right unless it is hulled and ground in the old way, and the blending of spices must have long and gentle simmering for the end result to be correct and lasting.

The art of making great varieties of cookery with combinations of corn, meats, beans, peppers, and powerful seasonings was a special talent of Mexican cooks.

23

MEXICAN-STYLE POT COFFEE

TO MAKE about 4 cups: Heat 4 cups water and add 1/2 cup piloncillo (a brown unrefined loaf sugar). Cook until the sugar is dissolved. Add 4 tablespoons regular grind coffee and allow the mixture to boil 1 minute. Remove from fire and stir well. Cover the pot and let it stand until the grounds have settled, about 3 or 4 minutes. Strain and serve at once.

MEXICAN CHOCOLATE

MEXICAN CHOCOLATE can be had in most Mexican food stores and in some supermarkets. If it is not obtainable, use the same amount of sweet chocolate called for in the following recipe and add 1/2 teaspoon cinnamon to the mixture. Some of the best cacao, or cocoa, came from the state of Tabasco in Mexico. In the early days of our cookery the settlers would grind the cacao bean on the metate. A fire under the metate helped to take out the grease from the bean and assured a smooth blend with other ingredients.

OLD-FASHIONED MEXICAN CHOCOLATE DRINK

TO MAKE about 6 servings: Grate 6 squares of Mexican chocolate and dissolve in 1/2 cup hot milk. Add 6 cups milk and boil for about 5 minutes. Remove from the fire and cool. Beat the yolks of 2 eggs and continue beating while combining the two mixtures. Beat all to a froth before serving. Sugar may be added according to taste. Serve hot or cold.

ROMPOPE: EGGNOG

ROMPOPE is a beverage based on milk and egg yolks, very much like our Christmas eggnog.

To make about 16 servings: Bring 4 cups sweet milk to a boil, add 1 1/2 cups sugar and 1 teaspoon vanilla. Remove from fire and cool. Beat the yolks of 8 eggs until light and lemon colored. Combine them slowly with the milk, stirring constantly. Return to the fire and bring to a boil once more but do not boil. Remove from heat, cool again and add 1 cup of Mexican liqueur—or 1 cup of bourbon. Strain and serve in liqueur glasses.

GARLIC DRESSING

NOW, once I saw an honest crook
And once a thin-man glutton
But never yet a buttonhole
To fit a garlic button.

To make approximately 1 1/2 cups: Blend 1/2 cup chili sauce with

1/4 cup white vinegar, 2 tablespoons sugar, 2 garlic buttons well-mashed, and 3/4 cup salad oil. Stir and beat until well blended. Chill before serving.

FRIED MASA

MASA, a corn product, is available in most Mexican food stores and in some of our supermarkets.

To make 6 to 8 servings: Prepare the mush by gradually adding 2 cups masa to 4 1/2 cups boiling water to which 1 teaspoon salt and 3 tablespoons bacon fat have been added. Cook for about 15 minutes, or until the mush is quite thick, stirring frequently. Remove from fire and pour into a buttered shallow baking dish, or pan. Place in refrigerator until the masa is completely set and can be cut easily. Cut into desired sizes, square or oblong, and fry in shallow hot bacon fat until brown, turning to brown on all sides. This bread can be served with a bean soup or with Mexican fried beans.

TAMALE PASTEL: TAMALE PIE

TO MAKE 4 to 6 servings: In 1 tablespoon lard sauté 1/2 cup chopped onion and 1 chopped garlic clove until tender. Add 1 pound cooked pork, cut into small pieces, 2 tablespoons chili powder, 1/4 teaspoon coriander, 1/2 teaspoon cumin, and salt to taste. Stir until blended and cook for 5 minutes. To this mixture add 1 cup canned tomatoes and 1/2 cup meat stock. Simmer for about 15 minutes. Bring 5 cups of water to a rolling boil, add 2 teaspoons salt, and gradually pour in 2 cups masa (or corn meal). Cook slowly for 10 minutes, or until thick, stirring frequently. Remove from heat, add 3 tablespoons bacon fat and pour about three-fourths of the mush into a well-buttered baking dish, pushing it around to line the sides and bottom of the dish. Spread the meat mixture over this and cover the top with the remaining mush. Bake in a slow oven, 325°, about one hour or until the pie is well blended and slightly brown.

TURKEY WITH TAMALE DRESSING

A 14 POUND DRESSED TURKEY with tamale dressing will serve 12 people generously. Three or four hours before roasting the turkey, rub it inside and out with a mixture of butter, lemon juice, and salt. When ready to roast, place the turkey in a large roaster which has a fitting lid and add 6 to 8 cups of water. Cover and bake for 2 hours at 375°. While it is roasting, prepare the dressing by mixing 6 cups of cornbread crumbs with 16 or 18 large husked tamales (use

either canned or freshly made ones). Add 4 beaten eggs, 2 table-spoons of grated onion, and blend well. Remove the turkey from the oven and dip off sufficient broth to moisten the dressing. You may either stuff the fowl with the dressing, or it can be baked separately in a well-buttered shallow baking pan. It should bake at least 45 minutes at 350°, or 30 minutes at 375°. Return the turkey to the oven and complete the roasting, about 2 hours or more, depending on the tenderness of the bird.

HOT CHALUPAS: PUEBLA STYLE

THIS is a modified version of a recipe, known as Hot Chalupas—Puebla Style, found in an old, old Mexican cookbook. They may be made with finely chopped beef, pork, mutton, or chicken meat. I prefer the chicken. The green sauce, made with green tomatoes, is most unusual, very tasty, and adds a most satisfying flavor to the finished product.

To make 4 to 6 servings: Use either commercial tortillas or, if you are real ambitious, make your own. But do allow at least two tortillas for each person. First, prepare the meat stuffing—which is chicken in this instance—for the tortillas by having 2 cups of boned, cooked chicken ready for use. Blend the chicken pieces with 2 cups of to-mato sauce, 1/4 teaspoon coriander, 1/4 teaspoon cumin, 1 table-spoon chili powder, and a sprinkle of salt. Cook this mixture over low heat for about 5 minutes or just until well blended. Soften the tortillas for rolling by dipping them in hot meat broth or frying them quickly on a hot buttered grill. Place 2 tablespoons of the chicken mixture on each tortilla and carefully wrap. Place them in a greased baking pan, seam side down, and cover with a sauce made as follows: Sauté 2 tablespoons grated onion in 2 tablespoons hot butter. Add 2 tablespoons minced jalapeña peppers and 1 cup finely chopped green tomatoes. (Canned tomatoes or fresh ones may be used.) Cook this sauce for about 5 minutes, then remove from the heat and add 1 cup sour cream and 1 cup chicken stock. Stir the sauce until completely smooth. Pour over the chalupas and bake in a moderate oven, 350°, for about 20 minutes. Just before removing from oven sprinkle them with 2 cups, or a little less, grated sharp cheese. Return to oven and bake until the cheese is well melted and the chalupas slightly brown. Wonderful and different!

NO DOUBT when the Indians first made tortillas they left them in the sun to dry for several hours before placing them near the fire to cook. I hope they had better luck keeping them intact than I have had. And I hope anyone trying to make them will make allowances for the amount of dough that sticks to the hands.

Mix 2 cups yellow corn meal with 1 teaspoon salt and sufficient warm water to make a very stiff dough. (A little flour may be added to make the handling easier.) Set the dough aside for about 30 minutes to rest. Wet the hands and mold the dough into balls the size of a walnut. Pat the balls into thin, very thin cakes. Bake on a lightly greased griddle, turning until the cake is slightly brown on both sides.

Tortillas can be made entirely of white flour, adding a teaspoon of baking powder and a small amount of lard. Also, masa can be used instead of regular corn meal.

TORTILLAS: CORN MEAL

WASH and pick over 2 cups frijoles, Mexican beans, and soak overnight. Drain them well, rinse and cover generously with cold water. Add 1/2 pound salt pork, 4 tablespoons chili powder, 1 teaspoon cumin, and a sprinkle of oregano. Boil slowly until tender, 4 to 6 hours. Many cooks prefer to let them simmer for as long as 8 hours, which adds greatly to their flavor. If the water boils away, and it may, add more boiling water, never cold. These are excellent served with chili, or served as a soup by adding more boiling water and 1/2 cup finely chopped onion about 1 hour before taking them from the fire.

MEXICAN BEANS: FRIJOLES

ALMOST EVERY PERSON who has lived *north of the border* in Texas, New Mexico, or Arizona for as long as five years has his or her own method of making chili con carne. And each person will give you his (without your asking) history or origin for the particular recipe. The following recipe is one that is found most often in homes of relatives of early settlers:

To make 6 to 8 servings: Cut 2 pounds of lean beef with a small amount of suet, and 1 pound of fresh pork into small cubes. Do not grind. In a saucepan in 2 tablespoons lard or bacon fat, brown one medium onion, finely chopped, and 2 garlic cloves, finely chopped. Stir into this mixture 1 teaspoon oregano, 1 teaspoon cumin powder, 6 tablespoons chili powder, which has been blended with 1 table-

CHILI CON CARNE

spoon flour. Add salt to taste and cook for about 5 minutes. Next, add the meat mixture and cook over low heat, covered, for 30 to 40 minutes or until the meat is very tender. Add 1 1/2 cups hot water or a little more, and cook 10 minutes longer. Serve without beans or with them, depending upon preference.

THE STORY OF CHILI SAUCE

THERE WAS A TIME when the Mexicans, the Indians, and the early Texas settlers gave chili sauce a great deal of credit for a large number of important influences on the human race. Some of them believed that the sauce, providing it was quite hot and strong, would protect one against colds, malaria, aid digestion and clarify the blood. There were other people who believed that it acted as a stimulant to the romantically inclined and helped to develop robustness and resistance to nature's adverse elements. Be that as it may, a basic chili sauce such as the following can serve many and varied purposes when cooking Mexican foods.

CHILI SAUCE

TO MAKE approximately 2 1/2 cups: Fry 4 tablespoons finely chopped onion and 1 chopped garlic clove in 3 tablespoons lard or bacon fat until tender. Blend 6 tablespoons of chili powder with 2 tablespoons flour, 1/2 teaspoon salt, and 1/2 teaspoon cumin powder. Add this to the onion mixture. Stir and cook for about 5 minutes. Gradually add 1 1/2 cups hot water, stirring constantly. When the mixture is well blended and smooth remove from the heat. If a thinner sauce is desired add a little more water. Serve this sauce hot over meats, tortillas, tomatoes, noodles, rice or over other Mexican dishes.

YELLOW SQUASH: MEXICAN STYLE

TO MAKE 4 to 6 servings: Sauté 1/2 cup minced onion and 1 minced garlic clove in 3 tablespoons bacon fat until the onion is tender. Add 2 tablespoons chili powder, 1/2 teaspoon coriander, and 1/4 teaspoon cumin powder and blend. Add 2 cups of canned tomatoes—the peeled variety—and cook the mixture slowly about 10 minutes. Prepare 2 pounds of very young and tender yellow summer squash for cooking, cutting them into 1 1/2 inch rounds. Drop them into the tomato sauce while it is still hot and cook the entire mixture until the squash is slightly tender, about 15 minutes. Add salt and cayenne pepper to taste and 2 teaspoons sugar. Blend well. Pour the mixture into a buttered casserole and top with 2 cups of grated cheese. Bake in a moderate oven, 350°, until the cheese is well melted and the entire mixture well blended. The finished product should be very moist but with very little excess liquid. The extra liquid may be spooned off.

ATOLE & CHOCOLATE

ATOLE is a corn gruel and may be served plain like the old-fashioned mush, or it can be made with a chocolate-sugar combination and served as a cereal or a pudding.

    To make 4 to 6 servings: Pour 1 cup of yellow corn meal in a shallow pan and set under the broiler to toast to a delicate brown, stirring frequently. Bring 2 1/2 cups water to a boil, add 1/2 teaspoon salt and slowly stir in 2 squares of Mexican chocolate (or use a sweet chocolate and a sprinkle of cinnamon). Blend well. Next add 3/4 cup sugar and the toasted meal. Cook for about 10 minutes, stirring constantly. Serve hot or cold. A dash of whipped cream adds glamour to this otherwise plain looking pudding.

SOPAIPILLAS: FRIED PUFFS

THESE WONDERFUL PUFFS may be used as a bread or one can make a sweet sauce and serve them as a dessert.

    To make 20 to 30 puffs: Sift 4 cups flour with 1 teaspoon baking powder and 1/2 teaspoon salt. Beat 2 eggs until light and add 1 cup sweet milk and 2 tablespoons melted lard. Combine the two mixtures —using only as much of the flour as the liquid will absorb. Roll the dough out as thin as possible. Cut it into desired sizes (or about 3 inches by 4 inches) and fry in deep hot fat until they are a delicate brown.

    When these puffs are served as a dessert they are usually cut into large rounds, with a hole pinched in the middle and then fried in hot deep fat. The dessert puffs are known as buñuelos.

MANGO CHIFFON PIE

THE MANGO, which is grown in abundance in Mexico, has been a great contribution to the diet of Texans who have been introduced to it. It is served in a variety of ways in our homes and in some restaurants, always with an exotic air. The canned ones, which are usually shipped into Texas from Mexico can be found in many small and exclusive grocery stores and often in supermarkets, especially in the southern part of the state. I find that the canned ones have a richer flavor than the fresh ones when used for cooking and are more practical when used in this particular pie recipe which follows.

To make one 9-inch mango chiffon pie: Prepare a 9-inch flaky baked pie crust ahead of time. Make a mango purée by running the fruit through a sieve to take out the fiber-like thread that is found in most of them. You will need 1 cup of the purée for this recipe. Dissolve 1 package (1 tablespoon) of unflavored gelatin in 1/4 cup water. Separate 3 eggs, beat the yolks until light, add 1/2 cup sugar and 1/2 cup sweet milk. Stir until blended. Cook this mixture over low heat, stirring constantly until it reaches the boiling point but do not let it boil. Add the gelatin and stir until completely dissolved. Add the purée and 2 tablespoons fresh lime juice. Refrigerate the mixture until it is almost thick. Beat the 3 egg whites until stiff, fold in 1/4 cup sugar, and add to the mixture. Refrigerate again until almost set. Beat 1 cup whipping cream until thick, fold half of it into the congealed pie, then pour the mixture into the baked crust and top with the remainder of the whipped cream. Garnish the top with shredded orange peel and chill several hours before serving. This pie freezes without loss of flavor if served within an hour or so after removing from freezer. *Elegante!*

GOAT'S MILK CHEESE

THE COOKS in a few of the small villages in Texas often prepare the following *goat cheese* recipe, or an adaptation, when they are preparing for big community dinners. Although I have never tried to make it, (I never seem to have any goat milk around), I have eaten it and found it most interesting and quite good.

Before junket or rennet tablets were available the cooks poured buttermilk into sweet goat's milk to start the clabbering process.

Crush one junket or rennet tablet and add to one gallon fresh goat's milk, which has been warmed. Allow this to stand in a warm place until a solid clabber is formed. This will take from 12 to 24 hours. Stir well and pour into cheesecloth bag. Allow this to hang where air can circulate around it. If possible, hang it outside so that it can drip onto the yard. It should hang until the whey is completely drained away. It must be quite dry. With the hands, mold it into a ball or into a flat cake. It may be served with cream and sugar, sprinkled with salt and black pepper, or with a dollop of sour cream.

THE NEW REPUBLIC

AFTER the colorful Mexican flag, with its powerful and lasting influence, came the exciting and history-making days of *The New Republic*. It was on April 21, 1836, under the leadership of the young General Sam Houston that Texas won a decisive victory over Mexico's Santa Anna at San Jacinto. This victory guaranteed the independence of The New Republic and although Texas lasted only ten years as an independent nation, she was recognized as such during this time by the United States, France, Germany, England, and certain minor powers.

With a stable government in control of the state's affairs, The New Republic began to make land grants and other attractive offers to the immigrants from European countries and to migrants from the older states in the Union. As these people came to the new country they brought with them not only their thrift, pioneer spirit, and ingenuity, but also seeds and plants for garden making. And with the resources for garden making they brought wonderful and varied ideas of their own cookery. As will be seen on the following pages, these spirited and energetic people made deep and lasting contributions to our cooking heritage.

The Scandinavians, the Polish and the Czechoslovakians settled mainly in the central sections of the state; the Germans made heavy settlements in the south central; the migrants from the older states of the Union and the Mexicans pushed to the west; the French moved into the east and southeast, and the New Republic took on a striking variety and complexity.

ASH CAKE, HOE CAKE, CORN DODGER

LIFE would have been intolerable many times for the early settlers had it not been for a basic food product, the *corn*. The pioneer cooks used this vegetable in countless ways and cooked it by many different methods, but one of the most satisfying and most often used ways was the bread, especially the simple and easy breads, such as the Ash Cake, the Hoe Cake, and the Corn Dodger.

These three cakes are a great deal alike in that they are made of a corn meal batter which is salted and made wet with cold or hot water.

The Ash Cake batter is cooked on either the hot hearth with hot ashes spread over the top, or out in the open spread between hot ashes. When the cake is brown the ashes are brushed off. Some of the ashes will penetrate the batter, but this only serves to enhance the flavor—or so the early settlers thought.

The Hoe Cake is the same batter cooked on a helveless (handleless) hoe. The batter is spread on the inside of the hoe and then propped up against the open blaze or placed directly in the hot ashes until brown.

Corn Dodger is the same batter made into small or large cakes, patted into rounds or oblongs with the hands and baked inside an oven on flat tins of some type. As the settlers were able to get a variety of food supplies they added bacon fat and eggs to the corn dodger. And finally they added soda or baking powder or both, making a light and tasty bread.

SOURDOUGH STARTER

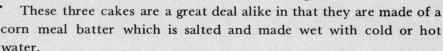

A COOKBOOK such as this would be incomplete without a recipe using sourdough. And a sourdough recipe would be incomplete without a recipe for sourdough starter. Most of the cookbooks before 1900 made reference to the bread starter but did not call it sourdough. It may be assumed, however, that the bread starter was about the same as this sourdough starter. My mother made her starter and yeast with a "handful" of hops added, but since I do not have a "handful" of hops, I make the starter by this recipe:

Soften 1 package of dry yeast in 1/2 cup lukewarm water. Add 1 tablespoon sugar and 1 teaspoon salt and 2 cups flour. Stir in sufficient warm water to make a thick batter. Set in a warm spot in the kitchen, cover, and let stand for 48 to 72 hours. At the end of this time the starter should have a pleasing sour odor. If the mixture separates and water comes to the top, think nothing of it; that is a part of the aging. To perpetuate, replace the amount of batter used each time with batter from the bread being made. The starter can be kept in the refrigerator after it once becomes sour.

SOURDOUGH BREAD

TO MAKE two medium-size loaves: Soften 1 package yeast in 1 1/2 cups lukewarm water. Add 1 cup of the sourdough starter, 4 cups flour and stir until well blended. If the dough becomes too thick to stir, use the hands and mix thoroughly. Place the dough in a greased bowl in a warm spot, cover and let rise until double in bulk, about 1 to 1 1/2 hours. When double, stir in or mix with hands 1 tablespoon salt, 2 tablespoons sugar, 1/2 teaspoon soda, and 1 cup, or more, of flour, or just as needed to prevent the dough from sticking to the hands and to keep it light and elastic. Turn out on a floured board and knead well. Shape into two oblong loaves, place on a greased cookie sheet, cover, and set in a warm place to double again. When ready to bake, brush with water and make diagonal slashes across the top with a sharp knife. Place a shallow pan of water in the oven with the bread. Bake at 400° until the crust is dark brown, about 35 minutes. Remove from oven and pan and brush with butter. The bread should be rather chewy and with just a hint of the sourdough flavor.

VANOČKY CZECHO-SLOVAKIAN COFFEE BREAD

THE RECIPE which follows was given to me by a friend whose mother brought it to Texas from Czechoslovakia more than sixty years ago. It was their Christmas cake and made with great respect for their traditional cookery. It is heavenly and could well be used for any holiday season or to replace the usual fruit cake.

To make the bread (cake): Cut 1/2 pound sweet cream butter, 1 cup sugar, and 1 tablespoon salt into 8 cups flour. It should resemble coarse meal when it is finished. Warm 2 cups milk but do not scald, and beat 3 eggs into it. Combine the two mixtures. Soften 3 yeast cakes in 1/2 cup warm water and stir into the flour mixture. Work the mixture into a firm dough, kneading it lightly on a floured board until it is smooth and elastic, about 10 minutes. Place in a floured bowl, cover, and set in a warm spot. Let rise until double, which will be from 2 to 3 hours. When doubled, add 1 cup sliced almonds, the grated rind of one large lemon, and 1 cup raisins. Work them into the dough on a board which is not floured, distributing them well. Di-

vide the dough into nine portions, making 4 large, 3 medium, and 2 small balls. Then roll the balls into ropes or twists, 4, 3, and 2. Place the 4 large twists in a greased baking pan; then the 3 twists on top of the 4, pressing the ends together to secure; then the 2 twists on top of the others, pressing the ends and securing. You will then have a pyramid of the twists or ropes. Place in a warm spot to rise again, covered, until almost double, about 2 hours. Before baking, brush the top and sides of the bread with a beaten egg. Bake for 1 hour or more, until the bread leaves the sides of the pan. Bake at 375° or, if the bread browns too quickly, reduce the heat to 350°. You may test the bread for doneness with a cake tester through the center of it. Remove the bread from the pan when it comes from the oven. Cool, brush with butter and dust with powdered sugar.

GERMAN NOODLES

THE PIONEER WOMEN taught their daughters to make these noodles as soon as they were old enough, or tall enough, to reach a work table. It was not hard work to them but great fun.

To make 6 to 8 servings: Sift 2 cups flour onto a pastry board and make a well in the center of the flour. Break one egg into the well, add 2 tablespoons warm water and 1/4 teaspoon salt. With the fingers work the mixture together, gradually adding about 1/2 cup warm water or just enough to make a very stiff dough, but very smooth. Divide the dough into 2 equal parts. Roll out as thin as possible. Cut into ribbons or strips and let it rest for 30 minutes. In a deep kettle have a generous amount of salty water boiling, or you may wish to use meat stock instead of the water. Drop the noodles into the liquid, a few at a time, and boil just until tender. Drain them, toss with melted butter and bread crumbs and serve hot.

To make green noodles, add 1/2 cup spinach purée to the first mixture and as much additional flour as is necessary to make a stiff dough.

POTATO DUMPLINGS: KLOESSE

THE DUMPLINGS made from this recipe are excellent cooked with sauerbraten by adding them to the sauerbraten gravy about 20 minutes before removing the meat from the oven. However, the gravy may be poured off the meat, the dumplings dropped into it and cooked separate from the roast.

To make 6 to 8 servings: Boil 4 large potatoes in their jackets until tender. Cook, peel, and mash. Add about 1 to 1 1/2 cups flour, 1 teaspoon salt, and one beaten egg. With hands, work the mixture into a dough, adding more or less flour as needed. Shape into dumplings about the size of a walnut and drop into a large kettle of boiling salted water. Cover and cook for about 15 minutes at a slow boil. These may be boiled in a meat stock for an extra rich flavor. When they are cooked through, remove them from the liquid with a slotted spoon and toss them in a little melted butter. Serve immediately.

To stuff the dumplings: Pat some of the dough out in the palm of the hand and lay about 1 teaspoon of some filling in it. Pinch the dumplings together and cook as directed above. For fillings: Use fried bacon crumbs with bits of onion; diced bits of ham; buttered bread crumbs; some grated cheese; and so on.

CHICKEN & CORN SOUP

TO MAKE 4 to 6 servings: Bring 4 cups chicken stock to a boil. Drop in 1 tablespoon finely chopped green pepper, 1 teaspoon grated onion, 1 cup whole kernel (canned or fresh) corn, and 1 cup chopped chicken meat. Reduce the heat and allow the soup to simmer for about 20 minutes. Season with salt and cayenne pepper to taste. If you prefer a thicker soup add a few small egg noodles about 10 minutes before taking it from the fire.

SWEDISH ALMOND MEAT BALLS

THIS is my modified version of an early Swedish meat ball recipe, and a very favorite one it is.

To make 6 to 8 servings: Select a good 2 pound chuck or rump roast and have it ground through the sausage plate for a slightly coarser grind than is generally used. Season with salt and black pepper to taste. Add 2 tablespoons Worcestershire sauce, 2 eggs, 1/2 cup uncooked rice, and 1/2 cup toasted chopped almonds. Blend well and form into small balls about 1 inch in diameter. In a deep roasting pan with a fitting lid, pour two 10-ounce cans of cream of chicken soup and 3 cups of water. Mix well. Into this soup drop the meat balls carefully. Cover the roaster and bake in a moderate oven, 325°, for about 1 hour, or until the meat is slightly pink and increased in size. Lift the balls out of the soup and serve over hot rice. They can also be served over cooked tiny noodles or toast. Delicious!

SAUERBRATEN

TO MAKE 8 to 10 servings: Lay a 4 or 5 pound roast, any good cut, in a deep earthen crock, or heavy bowl. Mix 2 cups sour cream, 1/2 cup vinegar, 1 cup water, 1/2 cup sliced onions, and 2 teaspoons thyme together and pour over the meat. Drop 2 bay leaves on top of the roast, cover, and refrigerate for 3 or 4 days, turning 2 or 3 times each day. At the end of this time drain the liquid from the roast and retain it to be used later. Place the roast in a heavy roasting pan with fitting lid, sprinkle with 2 or 3 tablespoons flour, a little salt, black pepper, and 1 cup water. Cover and bake in a moderate oven, 325°, until tender, basting and turning occasionally. Bake about 20 minutes per pound, testing along to check for tenderness. Strain the liquid which has been drained off at the beginning and thicken it with a little flour. Cook over slow heat until the gravy is smooth and slightly brown, stirring occasionally.

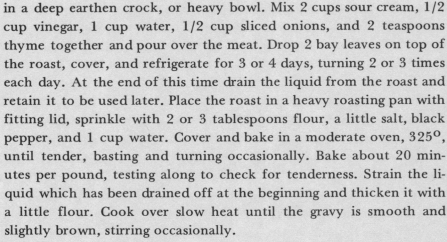

This is a good time to make potato dumplings (see potato dumpling recipe). They are excellent cooked in the gravy and served along with the sauerbraten.

POLISH MEAT PIES: PIEROGIS

ANY NUMBER of variations for fillings can be used in these tiny Polish pastry turnovers. Try cheese combinations or bacon and onions, and so on.

For the pastry: Beat 2 eggs into 1/2 cup water. Sift 2 cups flour with 1/2 teaspoon salt and gradually combine the two mixtures. Work it well into a firm dough. Cover and let rest for 20 minutes.

To prepare the filling: Sauté 3 tablespoons chopped onion in 2 tablespoons butter until tender. Add 1 1/2 cups cooked ground beef or pork, 1/2 cup chopped mushrooms, 3 tablespoons sour cream, and salt to taste.

Divide the dough into two portions and roll out to 1/4 inch thick. Cut into rounds 4 inches in diameter. Place 1 1/2 tablespoons filling on each round, moisten the edges, fold over and seal well, pressing the edges together with a fork. Drop the pierogis into boiling salted water and cook for 5 minutes. Drain them and remove to a buttered baking dish. Brush with beaten egg and bake in a moderate hot oven, 375°, for about 20 minutes or until brown.

To make a richer pierogis (turnover), pour the following sauce over them just before baking: Combine 4 tablespoons flour, 2 cups meat stock, 1 cup sour cream, 1 cup chopped mushrooms, and season with salt to taste.

THERE ARE few German restaurants in the state where one can still find this authentic hot potato salad served. It is certainly appreciated by those so fortunate as to discover it.

To make 4 to 6 servings: Boil 4 medium-size potatoes in their jackets until tender. Cool slightly, peel, dice and set aside. Heat 3 cups beef or chicken broth. Add to it 2 tablespoons finely chopped onion, 1 teaspoon celery seed, salt and pepper to taste. Since the broth will be salty already, very little seasoning will be needed; taste to make sure. Remove the broth from the heat and drop in the potatoes, allowing them to marinate in the mixture for about 30 minutes. While they are marinating, fry 2 slices of chopped bacon until crisp. Add 1/3 cup white vinegar, 1/3 cup water, 2 tablespoons sugar, and 2 tablespoons finely chopped sweet or sour pickles. Lift the potatoes from the broth with a slotted spoon and lay them in the skillet with the bacon mixture. Cover and cook slowly for about 5 minutes, or just until the potatoes are hot again. Lift them out of the liquid, sprinkle with paprika, and serve while hot.

HOT POTATO SALAD: GERMAN-STYLE

THE RECIPE given here for *Sweet and Sour Red Cabbage* is my version of a very old German one. There are many versions of this recipe and they can be found in homes in nearly all sections of the state; all the versions are "favorites."

To make 6 to 8 servings: Remove the outer leaves and hard core from a medium-size head of red cabbage and shred it into rather coarse pieces. In a large saucepan with a tight fitting lid cook 4 slices of chopped bacon and 1/2 cup chopped onion until the onion is tender. Pack the shredded cabbage into the saucepan on top of the onion and bacon, season with salt and black pepper to taste. Over this, pour 1/2 cup white vinegar, 1/2 cup water, 3/4 cup brown sugar (it must be *brown*) and 1 tart apple thinly sliced. Cover and cook slowly for about 1 1/2 hours or until the entire mixture is very tender and well blended. When ready to serve, lift the mixture out of whatever liquid might be left and serve hot.

SWEET & SOUR RED CABBAGE

THIS RECIPE has two distinct parts and special attention should be given to each. It is a time-consuming dish, but well worth the effort it takes since it can be frozen and reheated with success. In fact, the left-over is often better than the original.

HUNGARIAN CABBAGE ROLL

To make 6 to 8 servings: For the sauce melt 4 tablespoons butter, add 4 slices of chopped bacon and 1/2 cup finely chopped onion. Cook over a low heat until the onion is tender. Add 6 cups canned tomatoes, 1/4 teaspoon cayenne pepper, 1/2 teaspoon thyme, 2 teaspoons paprika, 1 tablespoon sesame seed, and 1/2 teaspoon nutmeg. Stir the mixture well and cook slowly for about 30 minutes, or until the seasonings are well blended. If the mixture does not have sufficient liquid to cover the rolls that will be added later, you may add a little water at a time until the desired quantity is reached. Just before the rolls are placed in the oven to bake add 2 or 3 bay leaves to the sauce and remove them before serving. Pour the sauce into a large roaster which has a fitting lid and set aside.

To make the rolls: Remove the stalk and the soiled outer leaves of a large head of fresh, crisp cabbage and drop it into a large kettle of boiling water. Let the cabbage boil for 2 or 3 minutes or until the outer leaves are soft enough to roll without breaking. Take them from the head carefully and drain on a cloth. Season 2 pounds of coarsely ground beef and 1/2 pound ground pork with salt and black pepper to taste. Add 2 eggs, 1/2 cup uncooked rice, and 4 tablespoons Worcestershire sauce, and blend well. Divide the meat mixture into desired number of portions and lay each portion on a separate cabbage leaf. Roll the leaf carefully, tucking in the sides to prevent the mixture from spilling. Arrange the rolls in the sauce, cover the roaster, and bake in a moderate oven, 325°, for about 1 hour, or a little longer. Test to see if the meat is cooked. Do not overcook. The rolls are excellent served with hot rice or with some of the sauce spooned over each roll.

POOR MAN'S CAKE: FATTIGMAND

THE SCANDINAVIANS called this recipe "poor man's cake," although it really isn't. They are, instead, wonderful little sweets much like our cookies and are best served while still very hot.

To make them: Separate 3 eggs, beating yolks slightly and whites until foamy, but not stiff. To the yolks add 3 tablespoons sugar, 6 tablespoons sweet cream, 1 teaspoon vanilla, 1/4 teaspoon ground cardamon, 1/4 teaspoon salt, and 2 tablespoons bourbon. Add the beaten whites and about 3 cups flour. The flour should be added gradually, using as little as possible but sufficient to make a soft dough that can be handled easily. Roll the dough thin (it should be rather rubbery and spring back), cut it into diamond shapes, cut a slit in the center and fry in deep hot lard. Remove them from the fat when they are golden brown, drain on paper and dust with powdered sugar.

DANISH SOUR CREAM COOKIES

THESE delicious little cookies are full of calories and very fattening. So, just maybe, you won't want to make them or eat them. However, I make them and we eat them and they're wonderful!

To make them: cream 2 cups of sugar with 1 cup of sweet cream butter, add 1/4 teaspoon salt, 1 cup sour cream, 1 teaspoon vanilla, 1/2 teaspoon grated lemon rind, and blend well. Add 2 eggs, well-beaten, and 1 teaspoon soda. Bind this mixture with sufficient flour to make a dough thick enough to roll but still soft, about 2 1/2 cups of flour. Roll the dough out to a 1/4 inch thickness, cut into any desired shape or size and bake on a greased cookie sheet for about 12 minutes, at 375°, until slightly brown. Dust them with powdered sugar as they come from the oven.

DANISH APPLE PUDDING

TO MAKE 4 to 6 servings: Sauté 1 1/2 cups fine bread crumbs in 1/3 cup hot butter until they are slightly brown. Mix 2 cups sweetened apple sauce, grated rind of 1 lemon, 1/2 teaspoon cinnamon, 1/2 cup nuts. In a buttered baking loaf pan spread first a layer of the bread crumbs, then a layer of the apple sauce, and so on, until all ingredients are used. The top layer should be bread crumbs. Dot the whole with butter and bake in a moderate oven, 350°, for about 30 minutes. Remove from oven and when cool, spread the top with 1/2 cup heavy cream whipped until stiff and sweetened with 2 tablespoons of powdered sugar. Dot the cream topping with small drops of some red jelly to give the pudding a bit of glamour.

TEXAS UNDER THE CONFEDERACY

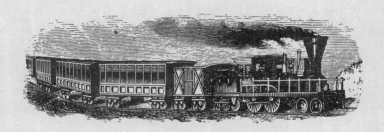

AT THE ONSET of the Civil War, the New Republic became involved in the dispute over the consuming and inflammable subject *slavery*. Texas had received an offer earlier, February 1845, of annexation by the United States government, which she readily accepted and by the end of that year had entered into the Union where she would remain until secession in 1861. But from 1861 to 1865 Texas was a part of the Confederacy. Other southern states seceded from the Union along with Texas at the same time.

During the Civil War, food was extremely scarce in most of the southern states. However, because the war was not fought within her boundaries, Texas was able to protect not only most of her food supplies, but ammunition as well. The military forces which were billeted in Texas during this period were said not only to have fought in platoons but also to have gotten drunk in platoons. When good liquor was not available, and this was often, they could usually find a supply of persimmon beer or "corn juice."

At the close of the war when money was almost impossible to get, many state officials camped out in their wagons in order to attend sessions of the legislature. One story reported that it was pretty humorous seeing an eloquent representative at work in the Senate Chamber all day and stirring up corn dodger or cooking slapjacks at evening time.

The foods most often mentioned during the Confederacy reign were the simple ones, such as wild game, hot breads, soups, custards, griddle cakes, wild berries and so on. However, even with the war

and its accompanying privations, the foods, the eating habits, and the particular methods of preparing the foods of the *Deep South* came *west* to stay during this period of our history.

HOW TO KEEP BUTTER SWEET FOR YEARS— 1856-STYLE

AS MENTIONED BEFORE, some of the fascinating directions, methods of cooking, quaint measurements and language used in the long-ago recipes make for such delightful reading that I want to include in this section some that belong to this particular period in our history. Of course, the reader will not be expected to follow the procedures given in these recipes, but he or she will find them interesting conversation bits as well as exciting reading. The several which follow are from old cookbooks which I am quoting as found.

To show the reader how the early pioneers used various methods to preserve their foods for months—or years—I am quoting this amazing "receipt" for keeping butter sweet for years. It is from *Godey's Lady's Book and Magazine,* 1856:

The butter must be well churned and worked and packed hard and tight in kegs of seasoned white oak; the head is put on, leaving a small hole, in which brine is poured to fill the vacant space; and of so much importance is it deemed to prevent any bad taste that the plug of the hole must not be made of cedar or pine, but of cypress or basswood; as otherwise it would be injured. After which these kegs are placed in hogshead well filled with brine of full solution that will bear an egg, which is then headed up tight and close. By adopting this process butter will keep in any climate for years.

Now! If you're interested in keeping some freshly churned butter for years, you'll want to follow this *receipt.*

SLAPJACKS— 1863

THE SLAPJACK was evidently one of the many forerunners of the modern-day pancake; however, this recipe which follows could be said to be the forerunner of just about anything. I found it in *The Old Confederacy Receipt Book,* 1863:

Take flour, little sugar and water, mix with or without a little yeast, the latter better if at hand, mix into paste and fry the same as fritters in clean fat.

FORTUNATELY for today's cooks that method went out of style years ago. For a newer version I like the following recipe for Slapjacks:

Sift 2 cups flour with 1 teaspoon salt and 1 tablespoon sugar. Scald 1 cup milk and cool. Soften 1 yeast cake, or package, in 1/4 cup warm water. Combine the mixtures. Beat in 2 eggs and let rise for 20 minutes. Stir down, add 3 tablespoons melted butter and drop 1 tablespoon at a time on a hot griddle to fry as pancakes.

How many will this recipe serve? Who knows? Try it and see—that was the manner of cookery in the days of the *Confederacy.*

THE FIRST TEXAS COOK BOOK, which was also known as *A Thorough Treatise on the Art of Cookery,* was published in 1883 by the First Presbyterian Church of Houston, Texas. It was edited by the Ladies Association of the Church, and many of the church's members made contributions to it. Some of the contributors gave their names with their contributions.

It is worth anyone's time and energy to read this fascinating cook book, and if you are fortunate you may find a copy of the Facsimile Edition, printed in Houston, December, 1963, in an occasional book store.

Some marvelous old gentleman, who signed his name Hon. J. C. Hutcheson, made a contribution to the above mentioned cookbook of the following recipe on *How to Cook Cornfield Peas:*

Go to the pea-patch early in the morning and gather the peas, take them home in a split basket. Take them in the left hand and gouge them out with your right thumb until it gets sore, then reverse hands. Look the pea well in the eye to see its color, but cook them anyway, as no color exempts the pea from domestic service, still the grey eye and white lips and cheeks are to be preferred. Throw the shelled peas mercilessly into hot water and boil them until they "cave in." When you see they are well subdued, take them out and fry them about ten minutes in gravy—plenty of gravy, good fat meat gravy, and try to induce the gravy to marry and become social with the peas. When you see that the union is complete, so that no man can put them asunder, and would not wish to if he could, put them in a dish and eat them all.

**AN OMELET—
1883**

ANOTHER interesting receipt from *The First Texas Cook Book*, 1883, was a contribution of a Mrs. D. C. Smith on how to make *an omelet*:

It is an easy thing to do and not often well done. The trouble lies in the fact that most cooks overbeat their eggs. A simple omelet is not a soufflé. Break all the eggs into one plate, stir rather than beat them, and to each three eggs used put in one teaspoon cold water. I do not like milk. Salt and pepper the eggs moderately *(American cooks use too much pepper)*, take some parsley and chop it. Let the parsley be fine—fine (American cooks never chop parsley fine enough), put two ounces of sweet butter in your pan—lard for an omelet is an abomination. When the butter is very hot, pour in the eggs; the instant that it is cooked on one side (crisp but simply cooked) turn it quickly and cook the other side. Double it over when you serve it, on a very hot plate. The cold water used makes the omelet light and moist.

**CORN
BATTER
CAKES—1883**

THIS CORN BATTER CAKE recipe is no doubt another early ancestor of the pancake, and how many the recipe will serve or what of the details of the makings—your guess is as good as mine. It comes also from *The First Texas Cook Book*, 1883:

One pint of corn meal, three-fourths pint of flour, one even teaspoon soda, one teaspoon of salt, one and half quarts of sweet milk, two or three eggs. Have a very hot griddle and grease with a piece of fat middling. Keep the cook in good humor, have a hot fire and turn quickly. One quart of water can be substituted in scarcity of milk.

**KISS
PUDDING—
1883**

A CONTRIBUTION from a Mrs. E. R. Falls to *The First Texas Cook Book*, 1883, is this *Kiss Pudding*. I am not sure what the name *kiss* has to do with the pudding, but who knows, perhaps if one can follow this recipe she deserves to be kissed.

One quart of milk, four tablespoons of corn starch, mixed with a little cold milk, five eggs. Beat the yolks of the eggs with one cup of sugar and the corn starch, put in the milk and let it boil until it thickens, stirring all the time. Beat the whites; add a cup of sugar, flavor and spread over the pudding and brown in the oven.

INGENIOUS and inventive methods used by the pioneer cooks in keeping foods for long periods of time is shown in this recipe found in a 1915 edition of *The White House Cook Book*, 1887.

Preserved Pumpkin: To each pound of pumpkin allow one pound of roughly pounded loaf sugar, one gill of lemon juice. Obtain a good, sweet pumpkin, halve it, take out the seeds and pare off the rind; cut it into neat slices. Weigh the pumpkin, put the slices in a pan or deep dish in layers, with the sugar sprinkled between them; pour the lemon juice over the top, and let the whole remain for two or three days. Boil all together, adding half a pint of water to every three pounds of sugar used, until the pumpkin becomes tender; then turn the whole into a pan where let it remain for a week; then drain off the syrup, boil it until it is quite thick, skim and pour it boiling over the pumpkin. A little bruised ginger and lemon rind, thinly pared, may be boiled in the syrup to flavor the pumpkin.

THIS RECIPE is given just to remind the readers of how early our grandmothers, or our great grandmothers, had to be up and about to prepare some of the so-called back-in-the-good-ole-days foods. It is also from the 1915 edition of *The White House Cook Book*, 1887:

Take one quart of dough from the bread at an early hour in the morning; break three eggs, separating yolks and whites, both to be whipped to a light froth; mix them into the dough and gradually add two tablespoons of melted butter, one of sugar, one teaspoonful of soda and enough warm milk with it until it is a batter the consistency of buckwheat cakes; beat it well and let it rise until breakfast time. Have the griddle hot and nicely greased, pour on the batter in small round cakes and bake to a light brown, the same as any griddle cake.

The "take one quart of dough from the bread" evidently referred to a "starter" similar to our sourdough starter.

THIS STUFFING RECIPE may be served as a casserole entrée as well as for stuffing a fowl.

To stuff a 4 to 6 pound fowl, chop the cooked giblets of a fowl and combine with 2 dozen oysters, which have been well drained. Add 1 cup oyster stock, 1 cup bread crumbs, 1/2 cup finely chopped onion, and 2 tablespoons melted butter. Stir all ingredients until well blended, then add 1/2 teaspoon sweet basil, 1/2 teaspoon rosemary,

and 1 teaspoon dry mustard. Stuff the fowl before it is roasted, or pour the stuffing into a well-greased baking pan and bake for about 30 minutes at 375°.

WILD DUCK STEW WITH TURNIPS

A DOMESTIC DUCK may be used for this recipe if a wild one is not available.

To make 6 to 8 servings: Cut 2 ducks into serving pieces and soak them an hour in a weak solution of vinegar and water to remove some of the wild flavor. In a large heavy kettle heat 2 tablespoons butter and sauté 1 cup chopped onion until tender. Remove the duck from the vinegar solution, rinse and wipe dry. Sprinkle each piece with salt, black pepper, dredge in flour, and place in the kettle with the onion mixture. Cover and cook over low heat, turning occasionally, until the pieces are slightly brown on all sides. Next, add 1 chopped garlic clove, 1 teaspoon thyme, and 1 bay leaf. Shake the pan to distribute the seasonings. Add 6 peeled turnips, cut into quarters. Add sufficient water to cover the entire stew. Cover and cook until the duck is completely tender. The turnips should be done by the same time. If an excess of fat appears on the stew, spoon it off from time to time as it cooks. A sprinkle of lemon juice over the duck pieces just before serving will add a delightful flavor.

CHITTER-LINGS: CHIT'LINS

CHITTERLINGS, known as "chit'lins" are a part of the small intestine of the hog. They are often available in some of the country meat shops in the state. They may be found in different forms, fresh, processed, smoked, or canned. There was a time in our history when the cooks made this recipe and called the result, *"Come to Texas Oysters."*

To make 4 to 6 servings: Wash 2 pounds of fresh chit'lins thoroughly and drop into boiling salted water, to which 1 green pepper and 1 teaspoon whole clove have been added. Cook until tender, then drain and cut the chit'lins into oyster-size pieces. Dip each piece in slightly beaten egg, then dredge in cracker crumbs. Fry in deep hot fat until brown. Drain on paper and serve hot.

FRIED RABBIT

IN THE EARLY DAYS the cooks were advised to wash the rabbit inside and out with vinegar "should it not be emptied immediately upon killing." Since wild rabbits are rarely eaten any more, we'll assume your rabbit has been properly "emptied." However, you'll find the flavor of the rabbit greatly enhanced it you soak the rabbit an hour or so in a weak solution of vinegar and water before frying.

Cut the rabbit into serving pieces, rinse thoroughly (or soak it in the solution mentioned above), and wipe dry. Sprinkle each piece with black pepper and salt. Dip the pieces in beaten egg, dredge in flour or bread crumbs. Drop into hot fat and cook until tender, turning as necessary to brown well on all sides. Serve with a slice of lemon on each piece.

VENISON STEAKS WITH APPLES

OUR FOREFATHERS had little or no worry about the "deer season"; for them it was twelve months long year in and year out. But the cooks did tire of feeding the family dried and stewed venison. They welcomed a change in its preparation as evidenced in this version of cooking venison.

To make 4 servings: Select 4 slices from a cut of venison which will broil quickly. Peel two cooking apples and cut them into thin slices. Lay the venison slices on a buttered broiling pan, sprinkle each with salt and black pepper to taste, and a dash of nutmeg. Place the apples on top of the venison, dot the whole with butter and broil, turning as necessary to brown on both sides. The venison can be served separate from the apples, adding sugar to the apples and serving them as a sauce.

MUTTON CHOPS WITH CURRANT JELLY

ALLOW one or two mutton chops for each person. Wipe the chops with a cloth dampened in brandy. Sprinkle each piece with salt. Dip in beaten egg yolk and dredge in flour. Fry until very tender in hot fat made from salt pork. Serve hot, with a teaspoon of currant jelly mixed with a pinch of dry mustard on each serving.

FRIED CHICKEN WITH HERBS

TO MAKE 4 to 6 servings: Cut up one 2-pound fryer into serving pieces, season with salt, black pepper, and dredge in flour. Cook in hot, not deep, fat until almost tender. Sprinkle with 1/2 teaspoon basil, 1/2 teaspoon thyme, 1 teaspoon paprika and pour over this 1 cup sour cream and 1/2 cup sweet milk. Cover and cook over low heat until the cooking is complete, basting often. The chicken should be very tender, the gravy a light brown and all of it of a delicate and satisfying flavor.

SOUTHERN FRIED CHICKEN

IT IS DOUBTFUL if any dish is as over-exposed and as poorly presented as the so-called *Southern Fried Chicken*. It can be one of the tastiest methods of preparing chicken, or it can be a complete flop. Real southern fried chicken is not loaded with a heavy crust, but has only a thin crust of flour, is very tender, moist, and cooked through and through.

The following recipe is my method of cooking *Southern Fried Chicken*—or the Texas method:

Use young fryers 1 1/2 to 2 pounds each. One such fryer should serve 4 persons generously. Wash the chickens thoroughly and pat dry with paper towels. Cut into serving pieces and sprinkle each with salt and pepper. Dredge in flour, or shake the pieces in a paper bag containing flour, salt, and pepper. In a heavy skillet with fitting lid, heat fresh vegetable shortening; never use leftover fat. The fat should be about 2 or 3 inches deep in the skillet after it has melted. Let the fat heat to the sizzling point but not to the smoking point. Drop in the pieces and fry for 5 or 6 minutes, turning at least once, then reduce the heat slightly. Cover with a heavy lid and continue frying at a constant heat without having the heat near the burning point. Turn as necessary to brown on all sides. When the pieces are brown and fork-tender, remove the lid and continue cooking just a few minutes longer, turning once more to dry and crisp the outside. Drain on brown paper and serve.

HOG JOWL & TURNIP GREENS

TRY IT! You may not like it—but some of us do!

Cook a cured hog jowl in slightly salty water until it is almost tender. Add one or more whole peeled onions, and fresh, crisp, well-washed turnip greens. (To make sure the greens do not retain tiny bugs, soak them for 30 minutes in real salty water and rinse well before adding to the cooking water.) A few sliced turnips should be included with the greens, and added about 30 minutes before the greens are to be removed from the fire. Cook the greens from 1 to 2 hours or until they are very tender. Drain them and serve on a hot platter with the cut-up jowl and the sliced turnips. The pot likker may be served in a separate dish—or how about as a gravy over hot cornbread?

TO STUFF a 3 to 4 pound chicken: Mix 4 cups cornbread crumbs with 3/4 cup finely chopped celery, 1/2 cup finely chopped onion, 3 eggs, salt and cayenne pepper to taste. Over this mixture pour sufficient broth from the chicken—which has been roasting—to make the mixture moist, but not soupy. Either stuff the chicken and return it to the oven to complete roasting, or bake the stuffing in a separate pan, allowing about 40 minutes, at 350°, for it to bake.

CORNBREAD STUFFING FOR CHICKEN

THE COOKS who live in the country still serve this rather interesting and unique dish quite often. But since green tomatoes are seldom found in our supermarkets, most of the city folk rarely have a chance to enjoy the tomato cooked in this manner.

GREEN TOMATO FRITTERS

To make 4 servings: Prepare 8 slices of green tomatoes by cutting them into approximately 1/4 inch thickness. Dip each slice in a batter made of beaten egg, 1/2 teaspoon sugar, salt and pepper to taste. Then dredge them in cornmeal or flour, fry in hot bacon fat, turning to brown on both sides. Drain on paper towels and serve hot.

TO MAKE 8 to 10 servings: Cook 2 cups hominy grits according to package directions. Just before removing from heat add 1/2 cup butter, 1/2 pound grated sharp cheese, 2 well beaten eggs, a dash of garlic salt, and 1/2 teaspoon cayenne pepper. Pour this mixture into a well-buttered casserole and bake at 400° for about 30 minutes or until slightly brown. The leftover may be chilled, cut into shapes and fried or baked in a very hot oven until brown.

GRITS SOUFFLÉ

TO MAKE 4 to 6 servings: Sift 2 cups flour with 3 teaspoons baking powder, 1 teaspoon salt. Add 3 tablespoons melted shortening, 2 tablespoons grated fresh onion, and 2/3 cup milk. This dough should be soft but stiff enough to pat or roll out on a floured board. Roll or pat the biscuits out to about 1/2 inch thick, cut into desired size, and bake on a greased cookie sheet at 400° until brown.

ONION BISCUITS

TO MAKE about 6 servings: Heat 2 cups sweet milk and gradually add 1 cup cornmeal. Cook until thick, stirring constantly. Remove from fire and add 2 well beaten eggs, 2 tablespoons butter, and 1/2 teaspoon salt. Pour the mixture into a greased baking dish and bake at 375° for about 30 minutes or until brown.

SPOON BREAD

CRACKLING CORNBREAD

CRACKLINGS—the skin or chunks of meat from the hog which has been rendered of all fat until the pieces are very crisp and almost dry. Crackling cornbread has been made in some form for many years and is still being made and appreciated today.

To make about 6 servings: Sift 1 1/2 cups cornmeal, 1/4 cup flour, 1/2 teaspoon soda, and 1 teaspoon salt. To this mixture add 2 cups buttermilk, 1 egg, and 1 cup finely chopped cracklings. Blend well. Pour the batter into a hot, well-greased, heavy baking pan and bake at 425° for about 25 minutes or until done.

MOLASSES STACK CAKE

THIS OLD RECIPE is supposed to have originated in the Carolinas. It was made in that area for years and somehow found its way to Texas, probably during the days of the Confederacy.

Blend together 1/2 cup buttermilk, 1/2 cup shortening, 1 egg, 1 cup molasses, 1/2 teaspoon soda, and a generous sprinkle of nutmeg and cinnamon. When these are blended to a smooth mixture, add sufficient flour—about 2 cups or a little more—to make a dough that will roll out. Roll the dough thin and cut it into round layers, the size of a small cake. Bake on a greased cookie sheet until slightly brown and thoroughly baked. Stack the layers by using a sweet and seasoned apple sauce between each layer. The top may have a little of the molasses dribbled over it—or the cake can be served with a dollop of whipped cream over it.

EGG COBBLER

AS EVIDENCE of the limited quantities and types of foods available to the early settlers, I am including this fascinating recipe. It was given to me by a friend whose husband's mother's mother gave it to her. Her husband is eighty years old! I have never tried to make it, although it must have had some merit "back when."

To make 6 to 8 servings: Line a large deep baking pan with pie crust. Into this crust break 12 eggs, being careful to keep them spread out on the bottom. Stack them only after the bottom is covered. Sprinkle over the eggs 1 to 1 1/2 cups sugar, spices such as cinnamon, nutmeg, and allspice. Next, dot with butter, using in all about 1/2 pound. Over this pour water until the eggs are barely covered. Cover the whole with a crust and a sprinkle of sugar and dot with butter on the top. Bake at 350° until brown. This can be served hot or cold.

ONLY GRANDMA or Grandma's Grandma could follow this recipe without some misgivings. However, some of the romantic sounding measurements used during this period of Texas history were really quite practical and certainly familiar to the housewife of that day. It is given here as it is said to have come down from a very old "receipt":

First, stoke the fire and lay in some wood. You'll need a moderate oven. Take 1 1/2 teacups butter, 2 blue cups sugar, 5 eggs, dropped in one at a time, and 5 handfuls flour. The cake will be fine and close with not a suspicion of any toughness or heaviness, not porous like a cake made light with gas from soda and cream of tartar.

Now, for those not brave enough to follow the old "receipt" above, here is a modern version (and I can assure you it is excellent). Beat 1 cup sweet cream butter with 1 2/3 cups sugar until smooth. Add 5 eggs, one at a time, and beat well after each addition. Next stir in 2 cups flour to which 1/2 teaspoon of mace, 1/2 teaspoon cream of tartar has been added. Stir in the grated rind of 1 lemon and blend well. Bake at 350° in a well greased and floured tube pan for about one hour or until the cake tests done.

THE UNION FOREVER

THE LAST FLAG to fly over the state, and the most glorious is that which signifies Texas as a part of the *Union Forever*, the flag of the United States. At the close of the Civil War in 1865, Texas wanted very much to keep her spot in the Union but it was not until 1870 that she was re-admitted into the Union to stay.

While the state was having its troubles becoming a stable and recognized part of the Union, her food was becoming more abundant and varied. Families were finding time to plant vegetable gardens and fruit trees. Wild game was still to be had for the shooting or trapping. Flour, sugar, coffee, and tea, although still very difficult to obtain at times, were an accepted part of the pioneer's pantry.

Thus, as the frontier faded into history, cookery, as any other civilized art, began to come into its own in the *Lone Star State*.

IN THE EARLY DAYS of our history the cooks made quick use of the first garden greens which appeared in the spring, as can be seen in this old recipe for soup.

SPRING SOUP

To make 4 servings: Take 4 cups of meat stock and combine with 2 tablespoons finely chopped onion, 1 cup fresh green peas, 1 cup chopped lettuce, and 2 well beaten egg yolks. Season with salt, pepper, and simmer until all ingredients are tender.

THE FOLLOWING is one of my *here-and-now* recipes on which the male and female guests are divided. The male guest says it is great; the female says it is fattening. And it may be.

CREAM OF BROCCOLI SOUP

To make 6 to 8 servings: In 2 cups of boiling water, cook 4 slices chopped bacon, 1/2 cup chopped onion, 1/2 cup chopped celery, 1/4 teaspoon cayenne pepper, and one 10-ounce package frozen broccoli, spears or chopped. Cook this mixture over low heat until all ingredients are very tender, almost mushy, about 30 minutes. With a wooden spoon force the mixture through a sieve or strainer to make a purée. In another saucepan, melt 4 tablespoons butter and blend in 4 tablespoons flour. Cook slowly, stirring constantly, until well blended and smooth. Gradually add 1 1/2 cups undiluted evaporated milk and 3 chicken bouillon cubes. Cook this mixture over low heat, stirring constantly, until the milk has absorbed the roux. Combine with the puree and heat but do not boil. Test for salt and other seasonings and correct as needed. The soup should be a delicate green, velvety, rich, and the consistency of a thick cream. Delicious!

CUCUMBER CHEESE MOLD

THIS is another of my *here-and-now* recipes which inspires division between the male and female guests. The male guest says "yuk" and the female guest says "yummy."

To make 6 to 8 servings: First, peel, remove large seeds, and grate 1 1/2 cups fresh, crisp cucumbers; add to this 1 tablespoon minced onion, sprinkle with salt, and set aside. In a large bowl, dissolve two 3-ounce packages of lime-flavored gelatin in 3 1/2 cups boiling water. Soften one 8-ounce package cream cheese and blend it with 1/2 cup mayonnaise. Combine this mixture with the gelatin while it is still hot. Stir, or blend until the mixture is completely smooth—and this isn't easy! Next, refrigerate the mixture until cool and almost set. Drain the cucumber and onion well and add to the gelatin and stir until the salad is well blended. Pour into one large or several small molds and refrigerate for several hours before serving. Poppy seed dressing adds a delightful finish for this wonderful salad. If a more colorful salad is desired, add 2 or 3 drops of green food coloring before refrigerating the salad the first time.

BLACK-EYED PEA SALAD

IN THE REST of the country, people say "black-eye peas." However, those of us who eat them most often say "black-eyed peas." Few cooks think of this rather plain vegetable being used in a guest-day dish. But it does make a delicious patio or picnic salad to accompany broiled steaks or barbecue meats.

To make 6 to 8 servings: In a large bowl, mix together 1/2 cup white vinegar, 1/3 cup sugar, with 1 cup salad oil, salt and pepper to taste. Add 4 cups of cooked, drained black-eyed peas. Place in refrigerator to marinate for at least 2 hours. When ready to complete the salad, add 1 tablespoon grated fresh onion, 1/2 cup minced sour or dill pickle, 2 tablespoons minced pimiento and 1/2 cup finely chopped celery. Toss the mixture lightly; it should not be mushy. To serve, lift the peas out of the liquid with a slotted spoon and onto a bed of lettuce. Garnish with tomato wedges.

THE FOLLOWING SALAD is excellent served with Mexican dishes when rice is not being used otherwise.

RICE SALAD

To serve 4 to 6: In a large bowl, mix together 1/2 cup white vinegar, 1/2 cup salad oil, 1/4 cup sugar, salt and pepper to taste. Add 3 cups dry and fluffy cooked rice. Place in refrigerator to marinate for at least 2 hours. At the end of this time remove the salad from refrigerator and add 3 tablespoons minced sweet pickle, 1/2 cup finely chopped celery, 3 tablespoons minced pimiento, 1 tablespoon grated fresh onion, and 2 tablespoons minced parsley. Toss the mixture lightly, and with a slotted spoon lift it out of the liquid and onto a bed of lettuce. Garnish with slices of cucumber, radishes, or tomato wedges.

THE METHOD of combining the *hunt* with whatever vegetables were available came from the Indians many years ago. It is an excellent way to make good use of the hunter's prize and serve a satisfying meal at the same time. There are several types of wild game that can be used in this recipe; however, I find that the wild fowl blends best with the vegetables. Try wild turkey, goose, duck, dove, or quail. In preparing the fowl for cooking after it is dressed, soak it a short time in a weak solution of vinegar and water. Then rinse it well and pat dry with paper towels. This will remove the flavor of feathers that is sometimes left on the wild birds.

HUNTER'S CHOWDER: INDIAN-STYLE

To make 6 to 8 servings: Have available at least 4 pounds of some wild fowl and prepare for cooking as directed above. Cut them into serving pieces and drop into a kettle of boiling water. The water should be sufficiently deep to cover the birds generously. Add 1 cup of sliced onions, 1/4 pound of sliced salt pork, black pepper and salt to taste. Cover and cook over low heat until the pieces are almost tender. Add 1 pound of fresh green beans and cook for a few minutes longer. Then add 4 cups of whole kernel corn, freshly cut from the cob. Complete the cooking and serve as you would a thick soup, in individual bowls.

GNOCCHI: TEXAS-STYLE

GNOCCHI, which had its origin in Europe years ago, has as its base either a cereal or a flour dough—and occasionally a base of potatoes. It can serve many purposes with many variations. The following recipe is one I worked out some time ago with my own variations. I call it *Texas-style Gnocchi*. You may want to use it as a bread, a foundation for some creamed meat, or as a base for hot chili (minus beans).

To make 4 to 6 servings: Cook 1 cup hominy grits in 4 cups of boiling water to which 3 chicken bouillon cubes have been added. Salt, if necessary, but only after tasting. Cook the grits according to package directions, stirring constantly until thick. Just before removing from the fire, add 4 tablespoons minced jalapeña peppers and 4 tablespoons butter. Pour into a well buttered shallow pan and chill for several hours. Cut into oblong pieces or any desired shapes, dip in a mixture of bread crumbs and parmesan cheese and fry in deep hot fat until brown. These may be placed on a buttered cookie sheet and browned quickly in a hot oven instead of frying. The oven should be at least 450°. If jalapeña peppers are not available use a green hot chili sauce and add gradually, tasting to get the desired seasoning.

SON-OF-A-GUN STEW

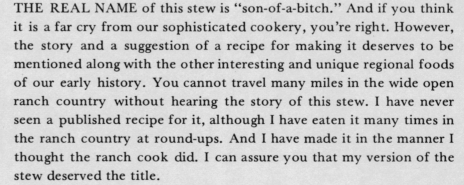

THE REAL NAME of this stew is "son-of-a-bitch." And if you think it is a far cry from our sophisticated cookery, you're right. However, the story and a suggestion of a recipe for making it deserves to be mentioned along with the other interesting and unique regional foods of our early history. You cannot travel many miles in the wide open ranch country without hearing the story of this stew. I have never seen a published recipe for it, although I have eaten it many times in the ranch country at round-ups. And I have made it in the manner I thought the ranch cook did. I can assure you that my version of the stew deserved the title.

If you asked a chuckwagon cook about the recipe he would tell you that the ranch hands or cowboys named the stew many years ago. He would also give you his "receipt" by saying that he made it with cheap, tough cuts of beef, pork, or mutton, or a combination of all three, added much water, tossed in 2 or 3 onions, 1 or 2 potatoes, some garlic, salt, pepper, and chili powder, then "boiled hell out of it." And *that* would be the story of *Son-of-a-Bitch Stew*.

RANCH-STYLE BEEF HASH

TO MAKE 4 to 6 servings: Into 4 cups beef stock add 1/2 cup chopped onion, 1/4 cup chopped green pepper, 1 minced garlic clove, 2 tablespoons chopped fresh red pepper, and 2 small potatoes, peeled and cubed. Cook this mixture until the onion and potatoes are almost tender. Drop in 2 cups cooked roast beef (or stewed beef) cut into 2 inch chunks. Add salt and pepper to taste. Cover the kettle and complete the cooking, about 10 minutes. Crackling cornbread goes well with this hash.

WILD DUCK WITH SAUERKRAUT

FOR 2 medium-sized wild ducks, prepare the stuffing by cooking together 4 cups of sauerkraut, 2 sliced apples, 4 slices of bacon cut into small pieces, until the mixture is blended, about 20 minutes. Wipe the ducks with a towel dipped in vinegar, then rinse them off. Stuff them with the sauerkraut, sprinkle with salt and pepper, lay strips of thinly sliced salt pork and thin slices of onion over the breasts of the ducks. Place them in a roaster which has a fitting lid, add 2 cups of water, cover and bake at 350° until tender. They should be basted from time to time as they are roasting. If too much fat appears as the ducks bake (and it may), spoon it off while basting.

ROAST QUAIL

THE GENEROUS COOK will allow at least one quail for each person. The birds should be dressed far enough ahead of time to allow them to cool thoroughly. When ready to bake, rub each bird with a mixture of lemon juice, salt, and butter. Arrange them in a roasting pan which has a fitting lid. Lay thin slices of bacon over the entire bird, sprinkle with a little meat broth. Add 2 or 3 cups of water to the roasting pan, depending on how many birds you are cooking. Cover and bake at 400° for about 30 or 40 minutes or until they are very tender. Remove the bacon and serve the birds whole—on a slice of toast.

BARBECUE SAUCE

EVERY COOKBOOK in the Southwest needs a barbecue sauce recipe. Therefore, I am including one of mine in this book.

To make about 2 cups: Mix 1/3 cup lemon juice, 1 tablespoon grated onion, 1 cup tomato catsup, 1/3 cup Worcestershire sauce, 1 cup water, 1 teaspoon chili powder, 1 teaspoon hot pepper sauce, 1 teaspoon sugar, and salt to taste. Add 2 minced garlic cloves if desired. Bring these ingredients to a boil, reduce the heat and simmer for about 15 minutes. When using this sauce for beef or chicken, add 2 or 3 tablespoons bacon fat. For pork, no extra fat is needed.

TUNA & CORN BAKE

TO MAKE 4 to 6 servings: In a large bowl mix together two 6-ounce cans of tuna, one 10-ounce can whole kernel corn, 2 eggs, 1 tablespoon grated onion, 4 tablespoons chopped pimiento, salt and pepper to taste. Blend well, then add 2 tablespoons Worcestershire sauce and 1/2 cup evaporated milk, undiluted. Stir again until all ingredients are well blended. Pour into a buttered shallow baking dish and spread several slices of sharp cheese over the top. Bake at 350° for about 30 minutes or until the mixture is thick and slightly brown.

BAKED CORN PUDDING

TO MAKE 4 to 6 servings: Blend 2 tablespoons flour with 2 tablespoons sugar and 4 tablespoons butter. When smooth add one 1-pound can creamed corn, 2 eggs, 1 cup sweet milk, 1 tablespoon minced onion, 1 tablespoon minced green pepper, 1 tablespoon minced pimiento, salt and black pepper to taste. Stir until well blended, then pour into buttered casserole dish; bake at 350° until well set and slightly brown.

CORN BALLS

TO MAKE 4 to 6 servings: Cut 2 cups fresh corn from cob, sprinkle with salt and black pepper to taste. Add 1 egg, 4 tablespoons melted butter, and sufficient flour to make a thick batter or dough that can be formed into tight balls. Use a tablespoon to measure the dough to keep the balls uniform in size. Roll and form the balls and dip in flour. Drop into hot bacon fat and cook until slightly brown, shaking the pan to turn the balls and keep them in shape. Drain on brown paper and serve hot.

FRIED OKRA

ALTHOUGH okra is not native to Texas, it is one of the most popular of the vegetables found in our diet. It is also well known that people who like it claim to "love it," and those who dislike it say they "hate it."

To make 2 to 4 servings: Wash 1 pound of fresh okra thoroughly, by taking the pods in the hands and making sure the tiny, sticky leaves are removed. Slice each pod into 1/3 inch rounds, snipping away the ends. Dip the pieces in a mixture of cornmeal, salt, and black pepper. Drop the slices into a frying pan of shallow hot bacon fat. Fry over medium heat, turning to prevent sticking, until the pods are tender and slightly brown, about 15 minutes. Prick with a fork to test tenderness. A tablespoon of grated onion is often added to the cornmeal mixture to enhance the flavor.

IT IS NOT KNOWN exactly when Texans began the custom of eating black-eyed peas on New Years Day for good luck. However, it has become a real fetish with many of the natives, and now we hear of people all over the Southwest observing this tradition with fervor. There are people who contend that one's future may be insured against misfortune just by being true to this custom. There was a time when the pioneers had little else in the larder, other than peas, which they often called "cow peas." Perhaps this situation helped to start the custom of eating them for *better* luck. To be really true to this custom, one is expected to serve them with cornbread, sliced salt pork and fresh onions.

NEW YEARS & BLACK-EYE PEAS

To make 6 generous servings: Wash and pick over 2 cups of dried black-eyed peas. Soak them for several hours before adding 1/4 pound salt pork, 1 or 2 onions, salt and black pepper to taste. Cover with boiling water and cook over medium heat for 2 or 3 hours until tender. Keep them covered during the cooking, but do not overcook them because they will become mushy. Serve with hot cornbread or hush puppies and a sprinkle of hot pepper sauce. If there are any left over, drain them well and fry in a bit of bacon fat, stirring and mashing until they are dry. For seasoning when serving them fried, add a dash of cayenne pepper or home made hot chili sauce.

FRIED APPLES at one time appeared on the breakfast table whenever they could be had. That's an eating custom that seems to have gone out of style. Too bad!

FRIED APPLES

59 : THE UNION FOREVER

To make 4 to 6 servings: Partially peel, core and cut 8 cooking apples into thin slices. Heat 4 tablespoons butter in a skillet and pour the apples into the hot fat. Pour over them about 1 cup sugar, depending on the tartness of the apples. Sprinkle with nutmeg or cinnamon, or both, add about 4 tablespoons water and cook slowly, turning occasionally, until they are tender and slightly brown. This old-fashioned dish is wonderful eaten with hot biscuits, pancakes, or waffles.

POTATO CRUST FOR MEAT PIES

TO MAKE crust sufficient for one 9-inch deep-dish pie: Boil 4 or 5 medium-size potatoes until tender. Cool and peel, mash very fine and set aside. When the potatoes have had time to dry slightly, mix with salt to taste (about 1 teaspoon), 3 tablespoons heavy cream, 1 egg yolk, and enough flour to make a dough that will roll. Roll out to about 1/4 inch thick. Use about 3/4 of the dough for lining a deep baking pan and fill the pan with any desired meat mixture. Use remaining dough to make a cover. Brush the top with melted butter and bake in a hot oven, 375°, until brown.

SOUR CREAM APPLE PIE

TO MAKE one 9-inch pie: Prepare one 9-inch unbaked pastry shell ahead of time. Sift 2 tablespoons flour with 1/4 teaspoon salt and 3/4 cup sugar. Stir in 1 unbeaten egg and 1 cup sour cream. Add 2 1/2 cups peeled and thinly sliced cooking apples. Pour this mixture into the unbaked pie shell and sprinkle with 1/2 teaspoon cinnamon and 1/4 teaspoon nutmeg. Bake in a hot oven, 375°, for about 15 minutes. Then reduce the heat to 350° and cook for 30 minutes longer or until the apples are quite tender. While the pie is baking, prepare a topping of 1 cup sugar mixed with 1/3 cup flour, 1 teaspoon cinnamon and 4 tablespoons butter. Sprinkle this mixture over top of pie and return to hot oven, 400°, for about 15 minutes to brown. An excellent dessert.

SWEET POTATO PIE

EVERY TEXAS COOK should have at least one *Sweet Potato Pie* recipe in her cookbooks. The one that follows can be used as a basic recipe and additions made to increase its flavor or glamour.

To make one 9-inch pie: Prepare one 9-inch unbaked pastry shell ahead of time. Season 1 cup of sweet potato purée with sugar, cinnamon, nutmeg, and vanilla to taste. Blend the mixture well. Stir in 1 cup sweet milk and 2 well beaten eggs. Add 4 tablespoons melted butter and pour the mixture into the unbaked crust. Bake at 400° for about 15 minutes, then reduce the heat to 350° and bake until the center of the pie is well set and the crust is brown.

SINCE pecans grow in abundance in our state, every cook either has her own version of a pecan pie or she will quote to you her mother's recipe. The following one is my own favorite. It is very rich and good.

TEXAS PECAN PIE

To make one 9-inch pie: Prepare the unbaked crust ahead. Combine 1 tablespoon cornmeal with 1/2 cup sugar. Beat 3 eggs until light and blend with cornmeal and sugar. Add 1 tablespoon white vinegar, 3/4 cup light corn syrup, 6 tablespoons butter, 1 teaspoon vanilla and 1 cup finely chopped pecan meats. Pour the mixture into the unbaked crust and bake in preheated oven at 425° for about 15 minutes or until slightly brown. Reduce the heat to 350° and bake for about 35 minutes or until the center of the pie is set.

TO MAKE about 24 small muffins: Cream together 1/2 cup butter and 1 cup sugar until smooth. Add 2 eggs, 1 cup ground raisins, the grated rind of 1 orange and beat or stir until blended. Sift 2 cups flour with 1 teaspoon soda and 1/4 teaspoon salt. Add the flour mixture with 3/4 cup buttermilk alternately to the first mixture. Blend until smooth. Bake in greased and floured muffin pans at 350° until done. As they come from the oven dip them in a mixture of 1/2 cup sugar and the juice of 1 orange.

PLANTATION ORANGE MUFFINS

DURING the exciting period of the expansion of the New Union, and as the frontier faded into history, the pioneers became very conscious of politics, government, and state affairs. This is evidenced by the names of some of the "receipts." The following is a recipe that was once known as "Republican Pudding." History doesn't tell us, but I assume that it was served with a "Democratic Sauce."

REPUBLICAN PUDDING

To make 4 to 6 servings: Scald 2 cups sweet milk, cool slightly, and add 1/2 cup sugar, 3 tablespoons butter, 3 eggs which have been beaten lightly. Stir in 1 cup cooked rice and 1 teaspoon vanilla. Blend all ingredients well. Pour into a well buttered baking pan and bake in a moderate oven, 350°, for about 30 minutes or until slightly brown. Serve hot or cold.

NUT BREAD

TO MAKE one medium-size loaf: Beat 2 eggs slightly, blend in 1 cup sugar and 3 tablespoons shortening. Sift 2 cups flour with 2 teaspoons baking powder, 1/2 teaspoon soda, 1/2 teaspoon salt, and combine with the egg mixture. Blend well but do not beat. Add 1 cup of chopped English walnuts or 1 cup of pecan meats and 1 teaspoon lemon flavoring. Blend this mixutre, add 1/2 cup orange juice and 1/4 cup water, and stir well. Pour into a greased and floured loaf pan and bake at 350° for about 30 minutes, or until the loaf tests done. This bread is excellent when it has cooled and is sliced thin and spread with cream cheese, butter, or with other cheese spreads.

CITRUS VALLEY TEA RINGS

THE USE of lemon rind and juice as the flavoring in this recipe is a delightful change from the usual cinnamon. It is a favorite with the "tea-coffee-time" people.

To make three medium-size rings: Dissolve 2 yeast cakes in 1/2 cup lukewarm water and set aside. Scald 1 cup of sweet milk and while it is still hot, add 2 tablespoons sugar, 4 tablespoons butter, 3 teaspoons salt, and stir until blended. When the mixture has reached room temperature, add the yeast and 2 eggs. Blend this mixture well. Add 4 cups flour, a little at a time—you may need more—and when the dough becomes too thick to stir, turn it out onto a floured board and knead lightly and quickly. Add enough flour to make the dough easy to handle and yet to keep it pliable. It should remain soft and light. Place the dough in a well greased deep bowl, cover, and set aside to rise until double in bulk, about 1 1/2 hours.

While the dough is rising, prepare the filling by blending together 1 cup brown sugar, 4 tablespoons butter, 1/3 cup lemon juice, the grated rind of one lemon and 3/4 cup chopped pecan meats. This mixture should be the consistency of a thick paste, but not too thick to spread evenly. Adjust the thickness by adding more lemon juice or sugar.

When the dough has doubled, divide it into three parts. Roll each part out to about 1/2 inch thickness and spread with a thin layer of the filling mixture. Fold the dough into cylinder-like shapes and lay each in a greased tube pan, surrounding the tube. Cover and let rise until double.

While the rings are rising, the topping may be prepared by mixing 2 1/2 cups confectioners sugar with 4 tablespoons butter, 3

to 4 tablespoons lemon juice and 1 egg yolk. Beat this mixture until smooth. Set aside. The mixture should be thick enough to spread easily.

When the rings have doubled, brush them generously with melted butter and bake in a 375° oven for about 30 minutes, or until they pull away from the sides of the pan. Remove from oven and spread the icing over tops and sides while the rings are still hot. The heat of the bread will cause the icing to become thin and syrupy, but as they cool, the icing will set and dry. Cut and eat a piece when you can stand the temptation no longer. You'll love it!

EAST TEXAS PECAN CAKE

THIS RECIPE came to me from a friend in East Texas with the title given here. Just why it is called *East* Texas Pecan Cake, I cannot say. Probably because the pecans grow in such abundance in that section of the state. This recipe makes an extra large cake and is a wonderful addition to the usual holiday cakes.

Cream 1/2 pound butter with 1 pound sugar until the mixture is light and smooth. Add the yolks of 6 eggs, one at a time, beating well after each addition. Sift 1 pound of flour with 2 teaspoons baking powder and gradually combine with 1 pound chopped dates, 1 pound chopped pecan meats, and 2 cups moist coconut. Blend this mixture with the butter mixture by hand. Beat 6 egg whites until stiff and fold into the total mixture. Just before baking add 4 ounces of lemon extract and stir until completely blended. Pour into a well-greased and floured tube pan, set the pan in a hot water bath—a large pan which has about 2 inches of water—in a 325° oven and bake for approximately 4 hours or until the cake tests done.

This very rich and delicious cake does not need an icing; however, it can be served with a sprinkle of powdered sugar or it can be topped with a hard sauce.

WHIZZER ROLLS

MY FRIENDS ask for this recipe calling it "Texas Fast Rolls." The name is not important, but the rolls are a delightful bread made in muffin pans and can be made from the beginning to the end in about 2 hours.

To make about 24 small bread muffins: Dissolve 1 package yeast in 1/4 cup warm water with 1 teaspoon sugar added. Scald 1/2 cup sweet milk and stir in 1/4 cup shortening, 1 tablespoon sugar, and 3

63 : THE UNION FOREVER

teaspoons salt. Set this mixture aside to cool. When it reaches room temperature, add the yeast, 2 eggs, and 2 1/2 cups flour or a little less, adding the flour a little at a time. Stir in the flour, beating by hand vigorously, and continue beating or stirring in the flour until the batter is thick but not too thick to stir—though it may take some effort. Set the dough in a warm place, cover, and let rise until double in bulk, about 3/4 hour. When the dough has doubled, stir it down with a wooden spoon until it is reduced to its original bulk. Spoon it into well greased muffin pans, filling each cup about one half full. Set aside again, covered with a cloth, in a warm place and let rise for about 30 minutes or until almost double again. Brush with melted butter and bake in a hot oven, 400°, for about 20 minutes or until brown and pulled away from sides of muffin cups. Brush again with melted butter and serve. For a nice variation and for party suppers, these may have 1/2 cup grated cheese and 1 tablespoon grated onion added to the batter before setting it aside to rise for the first time.

HUSH PUPPIES: THE STORY

THE STORY of *Hush Puppies* has been told for many years and in a dozen different ways. Just which story is to be considered authentic you will have to decide for yourself. But the way I heard it—when the early settlers camped out for the night to fish they would fry their catch over an open fire in a large heavy skillet. As the fish fried, a very thick batter of cornmeal, boiling water, salt, and sometimes chopped onion was made. The batter was dropped by large spoonsful into the skillet with the frying fish. The hungry hunting dogs stood nearby eyeing the preparation, yapping, growling, and being a nuisance in general. In order to stop the yapping, the cook would throw the dogs a glob of this hot cornbread and scream, *"Hush! Puppy! Hush!"* No doubt the cook added a few other loud and force-ful words along with the *hush, puppy, hush,* but we'll leave that to the reader's imagination.